GOD'S
UNTAPPED
RESOURCE

The Gifts Of The Spirit

Rev. Mario A Bruni, Dr. Div.

Leavitt Peak Press

ISBN: 978-1-961017-01-6 (sc)
ISBN: 978-1-961017-03-0 (hc)
ISBN: 978-1-961017-02-3 (e)

Rev. date: 04/05/2023

DEDICATION

I Maria J Bruni, do dedicate this book to the loving memory of my late husband and best friend for 49 ½ years Dr. Rev. Mario A Bruni. I thank the Lord Jesus Christ for saving us and anointing my husband to teach the Word of God. My husband's desire was to see the saints of God grounded in the Word of God, growing in their walk with God and being witnesses to the saving power of our Lord Jesus Christ.

CONTENTS

INTRODUCTION

In this new Millennium, the body of Christ will face many changes that are Christ oriented. These changes will come after God informs His Church about their coming; for "Surely the Lord GOD does nothing, unless He reveals His secret to His servants the prophets" (Amos 3:7). These changes that God will bring forth will bring division and strife to the body of Christ, but they are necessary for its purifying. Let us not forget Jesus will return for His Church so "that He might present it to Himself a glorious church, not having spot or wrinkle or any such thing, but that it [the Church] should be holy and without blemish" (Ephesians 5:27, KJV).

Many precious saints, because of unbelief, fear, and doubt, will be left far behind the move of God. They will miss many of the glorious blessings that are Spirit given. The most grievous result of this purifying will be the saints that will fall away because they are caught up in their own religiosity and traditions. These saints believe that God will not do anything different than what they have seen all their lives. They will sellout the move of God, perhaps even their salvation as well for the comfort of their dry and dead religious practices. "Do not remember the former things, nor consider the things of old. Behold, I will do a new thing. Now it shall spring forth; Shall you not know it?" (Isaiah 43:18-19a).

Take a good look at the world around us and at the Church of Jesus Christ. One thing stands out—God is shaking things up.

He is making major changes in our nation, in our world, in our climate, in our churches, and in our view of Him. God is using earthquakes, the weather, wars (both spiritual and physical), all kinds of tribulation, the educational system, TV, radio, the Internet, magazines, and newspapers to prepare the world and His Church for His soon return.

We are seeing in today's Church a great divide developing. On the one side, we have a polarization or an isolation movement. This movement is based upon strong and unbending, personal doctrinal beliefs which do not allow the love and grace of God to factor into their beliefs. On the other side, we see small isolated groups of ministers and ministries all across the world preaching unity. This movement of unity within the body of Christ is based on the belief that Jesus is the chief architect and cornerstone, and that his worldwide body of Christ should act just like our natural physical bodies, in which each part interacts, helping every other part for the betterment of the whole body. This group is looking for and establishing prayer meetings between congregations, denominations, and faiths.

These pastors are not restrictive. They do not isolate their congregations, but they allow their members to go and take part in other services using the strength of the other church to improve the spiritual and physical well being of the saints. This is the type of church that this minister believes will be the church of the twenty first century.

Today, we see ministries and ministers that are cookie cutter copies of each other. They look alike, talk alike, preach the same messages, and sing the same songs. Even the formats of the programs produced are the same. Their ministries are based on their past institutionalized learning and experience, not from fresh manna that is new every morning. They feel that if the idea or plan worked for one ministry, it will work for theirs. These ministers are depending on their presentation to attract people instead of the love, grace, and power of Christ. They substitute form, packaging, and advertising to cover up for the absence of Christ in their ministry. They produce their services and preach their messages so that it neatly fits into a pre-determined time and format.

These pastors do not allow the Holy Spirit to have His way, no matter the result or time needed. Their major concern is how many people they can reach or how large they can grow, which in itself is not wrong. But what is the reason for reaching them? Jesus is not concerned with the number of people that hear and recognize the preacher. He is concerned, however, with the number of people that hear and respond to the life changing power of the Gospel. Isn't the life changing Good News supposed to be the centerpiece of our work here on earth?

Nothing can be accomplished in the life of the unbeliever if the anointing of God is not present or the Gospel is not presented in purity and truth. Many more people will respond to the Gospel if ministers would spend more time communing with God than in board meetings discussing all the "how to's." Doesn't James tell us that "if any of you lacks wisdom, let him ask of God, who gives to all liberally and without reproach, and it will be given to him" (James 1:5)? And does not Acts 6:1-7 give us a God ordained pattern for today's pastoral ministry to follow? There is nothing wrong in asking for wisdom or direction in a board meeting. "A wise man will hear and increase learning, and a man of understanding will attain wise counsel" (Proverbs 1:5). "Where there is no counsel, the people fall; But in the multitude of counselors there is safety" (Proverbs 11:14). However, as good and biblical this is, it does not take the place of the wisdom gained by spending time with God asking for and obeying His counsel (Refer to Acts 6:1-7)

It Is the prayerful opinion of this minister that God is not limited to one style or program format. God is a God of diversity. He is as diverse as the number of stars in the sky or the infinite number of patterns found in snowflakes. How can so many ministries and ministers be doing, saying, and preaching the same messages, the same way over and over again with no real result? If these men and women of God were truly in touch with and obeying the Almighty, their messages and services would be just as fascinating, diversified, and filled with power as the first century church, and I dare say even more so!

Now some of you might be thinking that the messages we here today are the same because the message of the Gospel never changes. That is true. The Gospel never changes. The Gospel according to 1 Corinthians 15:1-4 is Jesus' death, burial, and resurrection that were witnessed by many. This Gospel message will never and should never change, for it is the Gospel message that brings life everlasting to each individual soul. The topics however, contained in the Gospel are innumerable and just as diversified. These Logos words, taken fresh off the Holy Altar of God every morning, are living, powerful, and sharper than any two-edged sword and will bring eternal life and health to the hearer (Hebrews 4:12).

There are too many ministers who are trying to be all they can be in the ministry. They are getting their glory and satisfaction out of the size of their ministries and the positions they hold. But, brethren, as long as Christians are concerned about whom they are in Christ, Christ can never become who He wants in them!

God is not only making great changes in the Church, but in the Christian as well. He is making those changes by shaking the very foundation of our faith. We must now get ready for it. If we don't, we may be shaken loose from the True Vine. The only way we can prepare for and maintain a firm grasp on Jesus and not be shaken loose, is through an intimate relationship with the Chief Cornerstone, the Author and Finisher of our faith, Jesus of Nazareth. This relationship comes through spending time, a lot of time, with Him in the quiet stillness of prayer (John 15:1-8). We must be able to recognize God's changes and be willing clay in the Potter's hand. This is what spending time, a lot of time, with Him in the quiet stillness of prayer will do.

We can also rest assured that the evil one will have a false call for change, a counterfeit of the true. Charles Caleb Colton once said "Imitation is the sincerest of flattery." As true as there is a devil, he will imitate the true move of God. This imitation, however, will lead naïve, comfortable, and unknowing saints away from the one true God into a form of godliness without the life giving Spirit. These imitations will be kept alive only by the devices that man's wisdom can manufacture (2 Timothy 3:5).

This God-ordained shaking will produce and establish a totally different Church, one that is active, productive, strong, and healthy, one filled with the power and Gifts of the Spirit. This new church will be totally evangelistic and world changing in nature; it will be a force the world will have to reckoned with but not be able to withstand. No longer will it stand around and passively accept the evil presented to it. It will destroy all the works of the devil, while ushering in the second return of its Glorified Lord.

We must all be ready to be molded into a devoted, moving, powerful, fully equipped, unified army that will make war against the devil and his principalities under one supreme leader, Jesus Christ. God is going to re-establish the Church the way He originally planned it to be. This last day's Church will be the same as it was in the beginning of the first century A.D.

Let me reemphasize what I believe God's plan is for the new millennium church:

1. The church will become a unified body working within itself and within all of its parts for the betterment of the Saints and the world.

2. God is going to reestablish the use of the Spiritual Gifts along with the ministries of the Apostle, Prophet, Evangelists, Pastors, and Teachers. These ministries will be filled with the Holy Ghost and be fully proficient in the Spiritual Gifts just like they were in the first century. These God called men will shake the Church and the world to its very foundation. Many of us will not like what they will say or do. We will be offended by them because the cancer of

pride which cries out, "Who is the greatest in the kingdom of Heaven?" is still running through the Church of Jesus Christ today (Matthew 18:1).

Many ministers believe they are in charge of their own ministries. Moreover, when God starts to make these changes, these ministers whether God called them to that ministry or not, will be removed if they don't change. God will put ministers who are after His own heart in their place in the same way that He replaced King Saul, a man who was called by God to lead Israel, with David, a man after God's own heart (See 1 Samuel 13:13-14; Acts13:21-22). These apostles, prophets, evangelists, pastors, and teachers, will not be men of renown but men who are simple and humble in heart. Their only thought will be of Christ and the establishment of His kingdom on earth.

In Matthew 18:1, the disciples asked a very interesting question, "Who then is greatest in the kingdom of heaven?" This question is still alive and well in the church today. Jesus' response to this question is most important to note.

He asked for a child to be brought to Him and said, "Verily I say unto you, except ye be converted, and become as little children, ye shall not enter into the kingdom of heaven. Whosoever therefore shall humble himself as this little child, the same is greatest in the kingdom of heaven" (Matthew 18:3-4). Beloved, a little child doesn't think of how he fits into the world, how great he is, or how much he has done for those around him. A child doesn't worry about how he is clothed or what color is his skin. A child is not concerned about the number of people that hear him or how and when he brings forth a message. The child's only concern is that someone responds to His message. As any of us that have children are painfully aware, children will unceasingly do anything and everything to make sure that there is a response to their message.

One more thing about children, all children require is to be fed, changed, and loved. As Christians, we need the same thing. We need to be fed with the Word of God, changed into God's image and likeness, and to be loved with an everlasting unchanging love that embraces and surrounds us. When all these requirements are met, they completely satisfy us. These brethren, is what Christ offers His children.

As we now begin to prepare ourselves for these upcoming changes, we will need to know our weapons, our gifts, our positions, our ministries, and our responsibilities in God's army. This means that it is an absolute necessity to understand who God is, how He operates, and through what means He will accomplish the work of bringing forth the new heavens and new earth. It is this minister's humble opinion that through a life of prayer, devotion to Christ, and through the Gifts of the Spirit that the new heavens and new earth will be accelerated and finally accomplished.

It is with this in mind that this book was written. May it prepare, encourage, and entice you to seek "Him who is able to keep you from stumbling, and to present you faultless before the presence of His glory with exceeding joy, to God our Savior, Who alone is wise, be glory and majesty, dominion and power, both now and forever; Amen" (Jude 1:24-25).

ARE THE GIFTS OF THE SPIRIT FOR TODAY?

F or the benefit of those precious saints that do not know what the Gifts of the Spirit are or where they can be found in the Word of God, listed below are the scripture references, a list of the Gifts, and why they were given to the church. The Gifts of the Spirit can be found in four passages in the New Testament:

1. Romans 12:3-8
2. 1 Corinthians 12:1-10, 28-31
3. Ephesians 4:11-12
4. 1 Peter 4:10-11

These are the Gifts of the Spirit as they appear in 1 Corinthians 12:1-10, 28-31 and Ephesians 4:11:

1. Word of Wisdom
2. Word of Knowledge
3. Faith
4. Gifts of Healing
5. Working of Miracles
6. Prophecy
7. Discerning of spirits
8. Different kinds of Tongues
9. Interpretation of Tongues
10. Apostles
11. Prophets

12. Teachers
13. Helps
14. Administrations
15. Evangelists
16. Pastors

Spiritual Gifts are those gifts given by God through the Holy Spirit. As with anything that is given to mankind by God, they have an important purpose. Listed below are the purposes for which they were given. According to Ephesians 4:12-17, they were given:

1. for the equipping of the saints for the work of ministry
2. for the edifying of the body of Christ
3. for the unity of the faith
4. for the knowledge of the Son of God
5. for becoming perfect (complete) men and women of God
6. for the measure of the stature of the fullness of Christ
7. so that we should no longer be children, tossed to and fro
8. so, we are not carried about with every wind of doctrine, by the trickery of men
9. for speaking the truth in love
10. to grow up in all things into Him who is the head – Christ
11. for effective working by which every part does its share
12. to cause growth in the body
13. for the edifying of itself in love
14. for the accomplishment of God's purpose in the world
15. for the edification of the church (the body of Christ, all the born-again believers)

There are four very important truths to remember about Spiritual Gifts before we begin to answer the question "Are the Gifts of the Spirit for today?"

1. Every believer has been given Spiritual Gifts (Romans 12:5-6, 1 Peter 4:10)
2. The Gifts belong to God and are freely given to the believer (1 Peter 4:11)
3. They are for edifying, equipping, and perfecting of the saints (Ephesians 4:12)
4. Spiritual Gifts are given on the basis of believing, not on the basis of works. For good or bad works will not qualify you or disqualify you from receiving the Spiritual Gifts, because they are freely given to man by the Holy Spirit (Mark 16:17).

Now to the task of answering the question "Are the Gifts of the Spirit for today?" To anyone who has read the New Testament, it is an undeniable fact that the Gifts of the Spirit were present in the early Church. There is an abundance of Scriptures that proves this beyond the shadow of a doubt. The question then, is not "Did they occupy a place in the early Church, but should they occupy a place in the Church today?" Such a question obviously deserves consideration, because if the Gifts of the Spirit were only for the Church of the past and are not a present-day reality, then how much more of the Scriptures were only for the Church of the past and are not a present-day reality? Therefore, if parts of the Bible only apply to the past, the question, then becomes, which parts.

If one holds to this train of thought, then only one conclusion can be reached, and that is that the Bible in its entirety is a good book, but not all of its precepts apply to today's society. This is the exact argument used by believers who hold to the teaching that the Gifts of the Spirit ceased, and by unbelievers trying to justify their sinful lifestyles. How easy would it be for someone to live according to God's precepts if they could just pick and choose which ones to obey?

Ask yourself' If salvation, sanctification, the new birth, His provision, or His love and mercy were only for the Church of the past and not a present-day reality, then where do we, as mere men, draw the line and say which part of God's inspired Word is for today? What formula do we use to make such a choice? With what part of man's obviously limited and flawed mentality do we choose? Is there any scientific evidence or proven method to support making such a choice? No, there is not! For no one can know and understand the infinite mind and purpose of God with our finite understanding. It takes faith and faith alone in every word He has preserved for us in the Bible.

Let me illustrate. Imagine you know of a priceless treasure that lies on the other side of a great gulf. The only way across this gulf is to walk across a bridge made of rope and wood. If, however, you do not cross the bridge you will never receive the treasure. Sounds easy, doesn't it? Just walk across the bridge. Here is the problem! You are not sure the bridge is trustworthy, or if each piece of wood you must step on is solid enough to support you, because, if any piece of wood gives way you will fall to your death. Herein lays the dilemma! What do you do? If you decide to walk across the bridge and you step on a bad board, you will fall to your death, however if you decide that, due to the danger, the prize is not worth your life you walk away disappointed. The third choice is to walk across the bridge believing the bridge is trustworthy and you can cross it and receive the priceless treasure. This is exactly the same with believing the Bible. Either it is completely solid and trustworthy or it is not! The eternal priceless treasure offered by God can only be obtained through believing God's road map, the Bible. If we doubt any part of it, the way becomes dangerous and we will miss out on our priceless treasure. God offers. The Bible leads us to God's bridge which bridges the gap between sinful man and a Holy God. The Bible's commands and precepts are the rope and boards. Christ Jesus is that bridge, and eternal life and peace is the priceless treasure that only He can give, for only in Him is eternal life (John 3:16; 1 John 5:20).

Christians must at all cost adhere to, trust in, and rely on the entire God given, God-breathed Word, we must hold fast to the conviction that it was given to the Church of the past as well as to the church of today. We must fully understand that, when we are reading God's Word or hearing a truly inspired message, we cannot put time restraints or limitations on it. We cannot say it was only for yesterday or it is only for today or even that it is prophetic and not for us now. God is beyond time. God is in today, the same as He is in tomorrow, just as He is in yesterday, all at the same time. Therefore, His entire word, which contains instructions developed from all these factors, is perfect. Knowing that and believing that God is love and works all things for our good allows us to have full faith in the quality, accuracy, and result of His precepts.

The answer to the question "Are the Gifts of the Spirit for today" is categorically yes! The Gifts of the Spirit are for today. "Jesus Christ is the same yesterday and today and forever! Stop being carried away by all kinds of unusual teachings, for it is good that the heart be strengthened by grace" (Hebrews 13:8-9a ISV).

Common sense would tell you that it is easier to have faith in God's entire Word then it would be to have faith in any one part of it. Wouldn't the doubt of, did I choose the right part to believe be with us all the way into eternity? What kind of peace and hope would that kind of faith bring? Or are eternity, peace, and hope, concepts only for the church of the past?

Christendom, for many centuries has believed that the Gifts of the Spirit should be regarded as the exclusive possession of the apostolic age. Many great and renowned scholars have held this view and have caused this view to be accepted with little reservation by both clergy and laity. It can also be concluded that these scholars have a number of fairly logical and, therefore, believable arguments to support their belief.

The proponents of this belief believe that supernatural signs and gifts were given to confirm the deity of the Lord Jesus and to give authenticity to the disciples and their message. Remember the church faced a hostile world. Jew and Gentile were united in their fierce opposition to the message given by Jesus, the Rabbi from Nazareth. It was necessary, therefore, that God supernaturally confirmed His message by signs and wonders in the name of His Holy child Jesus. It is doubtful whether the gospel could have gained a firm foothold in that "evil and adulterous generation" minus the miraculous signs. That is why these miraculous powers granted to the first preachers of the Gospel should be regarded as only temporary so that when their purpose had been fulfilled, they would then disappear from history.

Above all, advocates of this theory say that the completion of the Canon of Scripture (the Bible) removed all necessity for such extraordinary measures. From the time of its completion the church possessed the full and perfect revelation of God and His salvation plan. So, to desire a further revelation by any other means or to desire a confirmation of the Word by miraculous signs is to discredit the Word of God. In other words, God, who spoke in times past by miracles, speaks now only by His written Word.

One thing that is immediately obvious to every student of the Word about this teaching and even admitted by its advocates is the total absence of any definite declaration by the Lord of His intention to cause the Gifts of the Spirit to cease before His return.

Anyone that holds to the view that the Gifts of the Spirit are not for today must first successfully respond to the passage in Mark 16:15-20, which reads, "And He said to them, "Go into all the world and preach the gospel to every creature. He who believes and is baptized will be saved; but he who does not believe will be condemned. And these signs will follow those who believe: In My name they will cast out demons: they will speak with new tongues; they will take up serpents: and if they drink anything deadly, it will by no means hurt them, they will lay hands on the sick, and they will recover. So then, after the Lord had spoken to them, He was received up into heaven, and sat down at the right hand of God. And they went out and preached everywhere, the Lord working with them and confirming the word through the accompanying signs. Amen."

This passage contains a definite promise by the Lord Jesus, that these Gift shall follow anyone who believes. That promise by itself presents a severe and almost insurmountable problem to the assumption that the Gifts of the Spirit would cease before Jesus returns again.

One method used in dealing with the problem these verses pose is to question their authenticity to raise doubts as to their right to be included in the Canon of Scripture. The casting of doubt upon the genuineness of a portion of Scripture is quite a potent weapon. Even though there is no actual proof of its lack of genuineness, that portion of Scripture becomes so clouded with controversies that it births doubt and, as a result, loses its power as valid evidence. These ministers who hold this view have long used this tactic to remove passages which are distasteful to them.

Therefore, realizing the importance of establishing the authenticity of Mark 16:15-20, we offer the following arguments as proof of its authenticity:

1. The most ancient versions both of the Eastern and Western Churches, without a single exception, recognize this passage. The earliest version of the Vulgate called the "Old Italic," also contains this passage.

2. The evidence of Iranaeus (A.D.177). In one of his books (Adv. Haer.' iii.10) quotes the beginning and the end of Mark's Gospel in the same passage. The evidence of Iranaeus is conclusive as to the fact that, in his time, there was no doubt as to the genuineness and authenticity of the passage.

3. The question of the abrupt ending of the passage. The abruptness of the ending of verse eight is extremely striking in English, and still more so in the Greek. It seems scarcely possible to suppose that it could have ended there.

4. Knowing that Mark's Gospel was written to the Romans, it is highly doubtful that he would end his Gospel with the word "afraid." Mark 16:8 reads like this, "So they went out quickly and fled from the tomb, for they trembled and were amazed. And they said nothing to anyone, for they were afraid."

There are other arguments to refute the theory that the Gifts of the Spirit were only for the Church of the past. For example:

1. All the Spiritual Gifts hinge on one and only one thing believing. And now that we have given proof to the authenticity of Mark 16:15-20, let's look to whom the gifts are given as stated in Mark 16:17. The Gifts of the Spirit are given to all who believe. Therefore, the case of disproving that the Gifts of the Spirit are not for today falls on our opponents that must biblically prove when believing ceased?

2. 1 Corinthians 12:28 says, "And God has appointed these in the church: first apostles, second prophets, third teachers, after that miracles, then gifts of healings, helps, administrations, varieties of tongues." Paul obviously does not give any reference to the local church but to the universal church of Christ. Also, if we are to claim that healings are for yesterday, then why not claim that teachers and apostles and the Gifts of helps are also for yesterday. Is there anyone who can deny that the Church of Jesus Christ today has teachers or ministries of helps? No! They are as much a part of the Church as the pews you sit on. It stands to reason therefore, that the Gifts of healings and miracles also exist today.

3. How weak is a theory that must pull a portion of one verse out and leave in the other portion. Let's look at 1 Corinthians 13:8. It says, "Love never fails. But whether there are prophecies, they will fail; whether there are

tongues, they will cease; whether there is knowledge, it will vanish away." Verse 8 displays a contrast between the imperishable nature of God's love and that of Spiritual Gifts. If we use as an argument the first two parts of the verse to establish the passing away of the Gifts, then let us also use the third part of the verse to establish that the Gifts have not passed away. Let us note that the third part of the verse says, "whether there is knowledge, it will vanish away." Has knowledge vanished away? No. In fact, knowledge today is growing at a more rapid pace than at any time in the world's history.

4. According to Paul, when will the Gifts cease? 1 Corinthians 13:10 answers that question. "When that which is perfect has come, then that which is in part will be done away." Some of our opponents say the phrase "that which is perfect has come" refers to the Canon of Scripture, that which we call the Bible, and "that which is in part will be done away" refers to the Gifts of the Spirit. So, their argument is, when the Bible was completed, the Gifts ceased.

We also believe that the Bible is perfect and complete. However, notice what Paul says following this statement, "When I was a child, I spoke as a child; I understood as a child, I thought as a child; but when I became a man, I put away childish things. For now, we see in a mirror, dimly, but then face to face. Now I know in part, but then I shall know just as I also am known" (1 Corinthians 13:11-12). Notice especially verse 12, "For now we see in a mirror, dimly, but then face to face." Is Paul referring here to the Bible or, Jesus? The language is too plain to be interpreted in any other way than to mean Jesus. They are personal words, which can mean only one thing, seeing our glorified Lord as He now is. Is not Paul referring to the perfect age which will be ushered in by Jesus' soon coming? Or does this language suggest looking into the face of a book?

5. The Gifts are not mentioned in most of the New Testament so they must have ceased This argument is so ridiculous that it is hardly worth refuting. If something is not repeated in every epistle, does it make it false or temporary? No. If it were true, the Lord's Supper would also fall into the same category. The Lord's Supper is only mentioned in the Gospels and in the Corinthian letters.

6. 1 Corinthians 12:31 says, "...earnestly desire the best Gifts. And yet I show you a more excellent way." The more excellent way according to our opponents is Love. So, if Love is the more excellent way, then why do we need any of the Spiritual Gifts? As noble as that sounds, when do we assume that seeking a more excellent way, means in exclusion to anything else? Where do we get the idea that if we find God's true love, nothing else matters? Jesus was the embodiment of God's true love, and He still operated in all of the Gifts of the Spirit. Love is truly better than any of the Gifts—no argument there; except, one should not be completely ignored in order to obtain the other, for both are vital in order for us to come into the fullness of Christ. They are inseparably linked together. One cannot truly exist without the other, for when the true love of God exists in an individual, the Gifts inevitably appear as its evidence.

Please notice what the apostle Paul says in 1 Corinthians 14:1, "Pursue love, and desire spiritual gifts." According to the Apostle Paul, we are commanded to pursue both love and Spiritual Gifts, not to pursue love at the exclusion of the Spiritual Gifts. Notice that Paul does not say that we should seek Spiritual Gifts but to desire them. Desire is a strong word in the Greek language. It means to have a zeal for or to covet. The Authorized Version translates this passage, "desire to have spiritual gifts" (emphasis added). Now, notice what the results of the Gifts are for; edification, exhortation, and comfort. So, where do we get the idea that the church has no need of edification, exhortation, and comfort (1 Corinthians 14:3)? If you can see the church needing edification, exhortation, and comfort then you can see the Gifts still being in operation today.

Let's look once again at our opponents' reasons for the claim that the Gifts of the Spirit should be regarded as the exclusive possession of the apostolic age then compare them to what the world is like today in the Twenty First Century. That will help us to see if their reasons are valid. Their reasoning's are:

1. The supernatural signs and gifts were given to attest the deity of the Lord Jesus and to authenticate the disciples and their message.
2. The church faced a hostile world. Jew and Gentile were united in their fierce opposition to the Gospel of the crucified Nazarene. How necessary it was then that God should supernaturally confirm the message by stretching forth His hand to heal; and that signs and wonders might be done by the name of Jesus.
3. It is doubtful whether the Gospel ever could have gained a firm foothold in that "evil and adulterous generation" minus the miraculous signs.

The March 3, 1934, issue of the Sunday School Times carried an article from the book, Miraculous Healing, by Henry W. Frost, D.D., Home Director Emeritus for North America, China Inland Mission. In answering this question, Dr. Frost says, "Are signs still needed?" In answering this question,

> Two great facts are to be kept in mind. First, in the greater part of the world and among the largest number of people the Bible has never been circulated, and the missionary may make no appeal to it. Second, among Christianized peoples the

apostasy of Modernism has greatly undermined confidence in the authenticity of the Scriptures, so that the preachers appeal to it is largely none effective. The first of these facts brings us face to face with the condition which prevailed in Christ's day as a result of no enlightenment, and the second forces us to confront a similar condition as a result of unbelief.[1]

The Gospel of the Twenty First Century is still faced with a hostile and skeptical world. What fierce antagonism our missionaries encounter when they attempt to invade the strongholds of Judaism, Islam, Hinduism, Buddhism, etc. How strong is the opposition of the demon inspired followers of pagan religions the world over? Isn't unbelief widespread even in the so-called Christian nations of today? Do not Spiritualists, mediums who use Clairvoyance, and New Age teachers exercise an ever-increasing evil influence over the spirits of men? Is not antichristian activity multiplying everywhere? Then why should the Lord have decreed that the need of signs following His Word being preached would no longer be necessary, since the Church today is surrounded by conditions exactly the same faced by those of the First Century?

The Gifts of the Spirit were not given only for confirmation of the Word but to meet a definite physical, mental, or spiritual need. The mighty works of the Lord Jesus flowed out of a heart moved with compassion for the hungry multitudes, the loathsome leper, the deaf, the dumb, the blind, and the lame. This compassion was one of the main reasons for His continued miracles. "Jesus Christ is the same yesterday, today, and forever" (Hebrews 13:8). His love for the sick and their suffering has not grown cold. Wherever a need exists, He stands ready to meet that need. For this cause, He gave gifts unto men and confirmed the Word with signs following. What beneficial purposes the Gifts of the Spirit would serve in this world, where "the whole creation groans and labors with birth pangs together until now" (Romans 8:22 KJV)?

Friends, it would seem that the world in the Twenty First Century is not that much different, in respect to the need of the Gifts of the Spirit, as it was back in the First Century. The reason that the Gifts of the Spirit are disappearing or have disappeared altogether is not that the Lord decreed their removal because the Gifts are given "to all who believe." The disappearance of the Gifts lies not in God who made the promise but to the ones to whom the promise was given. The Gifts of the Spirit are disappearing because of Unbelief!

Here are the responses of some great men of God throughout church history, who were asked their opinion on why the Gifts of the Spirit have all but disappeared:

> The reason why many miracles are not now wrought is not so much because faith is established, as that unbelief reigns. —Johann Albrecht Bengel[2]

> It is the want of faith in our age which is the greatest hindrance to the stronger and more marked appearance of the miraculous power important reason for the retrogression of miracles. —Theodore Christlieb[3]

> Sapped in faith, in holiness, in aloofness from the world, the church relaxed its grasp of the Gifts, which, as manifestations of the Spirit, invited persecution; relied less on the Spirit, as it leaned more on the State; abandoned the powers of faith as it fell back to justification by works; until the divine and marvelous glory of the first splendid powers of faith was replaced by scarlet robes and crosses and censers of gold, and over the portal of

God's spiritual temple was inscribed Ichabod (the glory has departed). —D. M. Panton[4]

John Wesley lays the blame squarely on the church, telling us that the sign gifts decreased because: ...the love of many, almost all Christians so called, waxed cold. That was the real cause why the extraordinary gifts of the Holy Ghost were no longer to be found in the Christian Church: —John Wesley[5]

Dr. Harry A. Ironside expresses a similar thought. Some insist that these gifts have absolutely disappeared, but I do not know of any scripture that tells us that. I do not know of any scripture that says that the age of miracles is past, and I would not dare to say that the sign gifts all ended with Paul's imprisonment. I know from early church history that this is not true. —Dr. Harry A. Ironside[6]

If unbelief is the greatest hindrance to the Gifts being used today, then the second greatest hindrance is complacency. Let's look at 1 Thessalonians 5:16-22, which says, "Rejoice always, pray without ceasing, in everything give thanks; for this is the will of God in Christ Jesus for you. Do not quench the Spirit. Do not despise prophecies. Test all things; hold fast what is good. Abstain from every form of evil."

Did you notice what Paul says about the Spirit and the Gift of prophecy. "Do not quench the Spirit. Do not despise prophecies." These instructions are in the context of Paul's final instructions to the Thessalonians regarding the inevitable, unannounced, and soon second coming of the Lord (Ref. 1 Thessalonians 5; 1-4). Quite obviously, the church was not acting properly toward the movement of the Spirit and the Gifts that He brought with Him. That is the reason for Paul's admonishment.

The saints in Thessalonica had become complacent because they believed that the Lord's second coming could be at any time. The saints were becoming religious and mellow. The Holy Spirit's fire was going out, and with it, there was a growing resentment toward the saints that were still on fire and operating in the Spirit's power. Complacency and resentment are causing the Church to cease all the activities necessary for maintaining a strong and vital walk with the Lord. Paul, seeing the complacency gave the commands listed in 1 Thessalonians 5;16-22.

The third great hindrance for the disappearing of the Gifts of the Spirit is fear: fear of what you ask, fear that the Gifts are not in fact from God, fear of losing control of the service, fear of losing parishioners that don't understand, fear due to unbelief, fear of emotionalism, fear of conviction, and perhaps the most frightful is the fear of what might be revealed.

Let me give you some examples to illustrate my point. We had been attending a certain church on and off for about a year, and it occurred to me that at no time were the Gifts of the Spirit in operation. This church was Pentecostal in its beliefs, but there was no evidence of the Gifts in operation in the services. The Word of God was preached with power, people were getting saved on a regular basis, there was on going prayer for the sick and for the needs of the parishioners, but no Spiritual Gifts. Until one service, when the praise was glorious and the Spirit of God fell on the congregation so powerfully that many in the congregation were going to the altar in tears crying out in repentance, then it happened. One woman in the front pew started to prophesy. Immediately, the pastor got up, went to the pulpit, and tried to stop her by speaking over her to the congregation. When that did not work, he gestured to the ushers to restrain her. At first, this minister was startled at what was happening, but when I noticed the face of the pastor, the understanding was made clear. This man of God, who had been ministering for over fifty years, was struck with fear.

When the ushers could not stop her, the pastor spoke even louder trying to calm the woman down, and also trying (ineptly I might add) to explain to the congregation what was happening. When the prophecy had ended, the woman was escorted out of the sanctuary by the ushers. Since then, there has not been a single movement of the Gifts in that church. No matter what the pastor's fear stemmed from, it was present in the pastor's heart and his reasons for it are for God to judge. The fear that this man expressed, however, was so real and evident that anyone could have recognized it.

One other time, my wife and I were attending a church service at an Assembly of God church in Pennsylvania. At the beginning of the service, the congregation was instructed (I suppose for the sake of the visitors) that if anyone had a word from the Lord, such as a prophecy, tongues, or interpretation of tongues, they were to call the usher after writing it down on paper, and the usher would bring it to the front. It would then be judged. If it was determined to be from God, it would then be presented to the congregation. This quenched the Spirit of God from moving. The service was void of any kind of life, but the program schedule went smooth, each phase was perfectly on time, every person having their job down exactly right, every person being where they were to be at the right moment, and we were all dismissed right on time. The entire service took exactly sixty minutes.

How much is the body of Christ missing because the Gifts are being suppressed by unbelief, complacency, and fear? Remember, the Gifts of the Spirit are for edification, purification, exhortation, and for the perfecting (maturing) of the saints. When we eliminate any device that helps us achieve those ends, the results are disastrous. The church stays immature, weak, and vulnerable, tossed to and fro by Satan's wiles, and by every wind of doctrine. If there is any doubt about this truth, look at the Church of Jesus Christ today as a whole. We are not exactly turning the world upside down with the gospel, now are we?

Friends, the promise God made concerning the Gifts of the Spirit and their use is to "all who believe" (Mark 16:17). If you "believe," you are eligible for their manifestation in your life, not only to receive from them but also to use them for the betterment of all saints. Let us be confronted with the fact that it is the unbelief, complacency, and fear in our churches and in ourselves that have caused these Gifts to all but disappear. They were never meant to cease. Let us not accept the mistaken assumption that the Gifts of the Spirit were the exclusive possession of the apostolic age, simply because all major ecclesiastical bodies have embraced it and they are not prevalent in the Church today. For one thousand years of Church history 500-1500 A.D., the doctrine of justification by faith was not embraced by any major ecclesiastical body either. Let us now cry out to Christ with heartfelt tears, just like the father of the demon possessed boy "Lord, I believe; help thou my unbelief" (Mark 9:24, KJV).

Chapter Questions To Help Your Study

1. Spiritual Gifts or the Gifts of the Spirit are mentioned in four passages in the New Testament. What arc those four passages?
2. Spiritual Gifts are those gifts given by God through the Holy Spirit, for the accomplishment of God's purpose in the world and for the edification of the church (the body of Christ, all the born-again believers). True or False
3. There are four very important truths to remember about Spiritual Gifts. What are they?
4. Are the Gifts of the Spirit for today? Yes or No
5. What are two reasons why proponents of the belief that Spiritual Gifts are not for today, use to prove their point.
6. Is there even one definite declaration in the Word of God that the Spiritual Gifts were to cease? Yes or No
7. Anyone that holds to the view that the Gifts of the Spirit is not for today must first successfully answer what passage or he reduced to silence?
8. If the Gifts hinge on one and only one thing, what is it?
9. According to Paul, when will the Gifts cease?
10. The reason that the Gifts of the Spirit are disappearing or have disappeared today is because of what three factors?

TONGUES IN REGARDS TO THE BAPTISM OF THE HOLY SPIRIT

For all the readers that might be wondering why this chapter is included in this book, I offer this explanation. Many devoted and loving Christian brothers and sisters are under the misunderstanding that Tongues in regard to the Baptism of the Holy Spirit and the Gift of Tongues listed in 1 Corinthians 12:8-11 are one and the same. They are not! Even though they are both gifts, both given by the same Spirit, both supernatural, and even though the Gift of Tongues uses the initial tongue received at the baptism of the Holy Spirit, they are not the same! They are two distinct gifts. They are given for two totally different purposes.

The Gift of Tongues which is listed in 1 Corinthians 12:8-11 with the accompanying Gift of Interpretation is a gift given, not for personal use, but for unbelievers (1 Corinthians 14:20–25) to demonstrate that God is truly in the midst of His people (1 Corinthians 14:25b). This is in contrast to Tongues in regard to the baptism of the Holy Spirit, which is a personal gift. It is to help in personal edification (1 Corinthians 14:4). It is to help in our personal prayer life. It's for personal communication with the Father. It helps us to glorify and magnify God. It gives us power from on high to be witnesses for Him (Acts 1:8), and it gives strength to live a holy and fulfilling life.

Now, let us examine Tongues in regard to the baptism of the Holy Spirit more closely. This Gift according to the late Dr. R. A. Torrey is:

1. An operation of the Holy Spirit distinct from, subsequent, and additional to, His regenerating work.
2. An impartation of power and the one who receives it is fitted for service.
3. Not merely for the apostles, nor merely for those of the apostolic age, but for all that are afar off, even as many as the Lord our God shall call, as well; i.e. it is for every believer in every age of the church's history.[7]

According to the late Harold Horton, the Gift of Divers Kinds of Tongues, or speaking with tongues, is:

> The supernatural utterance by the Holy Spirit in languages never learned by the speaker—not understood by the mind of the speaker—nearly always not understood by the hearer. It has nothing to do with linguistic ability, nor with the mind of man or intellect of man. It is a manifestation of the mind of the Spirit of God employing human speech organs. The linguistic skill of man is no more employed in speaking with tongues than the surgical skill of man was employed when at Peter's word, "Rise and walk," the lame man instantly arose and walked (Acts 3:6).[8]

Therefore, we believe that He, who desires to endue us with power from on high has also provided an immediate means by which we can know whether or not we have received that endowment; i.e. by speaking with other tongues as the Spirit gives utterance (Acts 2:4).

The propagation of this doctrine has provoked a fierce, theological controversy in the ranks of Christianity. Many have urged Pentecostals to cease the spread of such a controversial doctrine, since it provokes so much strife, division, and unrest in the Body of Christ. What these brethren fail to realize is that in our insistence upon tongues (glossolalia, in the Greek), we are not contending for a pet doctrine but for that wonderful experience of which speaking with tongues is the initial, physical evidence. It is our sincere belief that without the evidence of speaking with other tongues as the Spirit gives utterance, there can be no fully Scriptural baptism in the Holy Spirit. Now whether we are right or wrong in this belief—you will have ample opportunity to decide as you examine the facts contained in this chapter.

Now let's get to the "glossolalia" itself. As stated, earlier, Tongues is the initial, physical evidence of the baptism of the Holy Spirit. The supernatural utterance by the Holy Spirit in languages never learned by the speaker—not understood by the mind of the speaker and nearly always not understood by the hearer. In John 7:37-38, the Lord Jesus said, "On the last day, that great day of the feast, Jesus stood and cried out, saying, 'If anyone thirsts, let him come to Me and drink.' He who believes in Me, as the Scripture has said, out of his heart will flow rivers of living water."

John adds this note in verse 39, "But this He spoke concerning the Spirit, whom those believing in Him would receive; for the Holy Spirit was not yet given, because Jesus was not yet glorified". These verses definitely point to Pentecost, as the apostle Peter declared in his Pentecost sermon, "Therefore being exalted to the right hand of God, and having received from the Father the promise of the Holy Spirit, He poured out this which you now see and hear" (Acts 2:33)

> Accordingly, we read in Acts 2:1-4,
> "When the Day of Pentecost had fully come, they were all with one accord in one place. And suddenly there came a sound from heaven, as of a rushing mighty wind, and it filled the whole house where they were sitting. Then there appeared to them divided tongues, as of fire, and one sat upon each

of them. And they were all filled with the Holy
Spirit and began to speak with other tongues, as
the Spirit gave them utterance."

These verses make it fairly easy to see that tongues are the
initial, physical evidence of the baptism of the Holy Spirit.

Now, let's look at some different aspects in regard to Baptism
in the Holy Spirit with the evidence of speaking in tongues:

1. It is personal in nature.
   Tongues is a direct communication between God and
   man. John the Baptist showed the personal nature of this
   experience by saying, "He shall baptize you with the Holy
   Ghost" (Matthew 3:11, Luke 3:16). Notice once again Acts
   2:4, which says, "they were all filled with the Holy Spirit and
   began to speak with other tongues, as the Spirit gave them
   utterance." Notice, speaking with other tongues was as the
   "Spirit gave them utterance." Understanding that the Holy
   Spirit is a real person, the third person in the Godhead,
   demonstrates the personal nature of the baptism. Every
   believer throughout the Church Age who has received this
   promise can testify that it has conformed to that of the one
   hundred and twenty at Pentecost in this regard; i.e. it has
   brought them into personal contact with the Lord Jesus.

2. It is for a specific purpose.
   Jesus established the purpose of the baptism or being filled
   with the Spirit in Luke 24:49: "Behold, I send the promise
   of my father upon you; but tarry in the city of Jerusalem
   until you are endued with power from on high." In Acts
   1:8, we read, "But you shall receive power when the Holy
   Spirit has come upon you; and you shall be witnesses to
   me in Jerusalem, and in all Judea and Samaria, and to the
   end of the earth." We are to receive power from on high.
   This word "power" is the word "Dunamis" in the Greek
   and it means the power or ability, which resides in every

person to do that which is beyond the physical ability of that individual, i.e. when performing miracles. Other meanings of the word are abundance, might, strength, and work. Notice what the Baptism of the Holy Spirit with the initial evidence of speaking in tongues is for, "and you shall be witnesses to me" (Acts 1:8).

So that there is no misunderstanding with many Pentecostal and non-Pentecostal students of the Word, we agree that the primary (we did not say the only) (Emphasis added) purpose of the baptism of the Holy Spirit, with the initial evidence of speaking with other tongues, is the endowment of believers with "power from on high." However, we believe that this power was not given for any personal or private purpose. This power was given so that we, as God's ambassadors, can be effective witnesses throughout the world.

3. It is the evidence of the Baptism.
   A. It is a matter of record that the experience at Pentecost was a charismatic one producing extraordinary effects, which were visible to onlookers, and where the initial baptism was shown to all as utterances never learned by them. It is our belief that speaking in tongues on that occasion formed the pattern for every similar baptism or charismatic endowment. For example, the reception of the Spirit by Cornelius and his household in Acts 10 was described by the Apostle Peter in these words, "... the Holy Ghost fell on them, as on us at the beginning" (Acts 11:15, 15:8). Also Acts 8:17-19; "Then they laid hands on Simon saw that through the laying on of the apostles' hands the Holy Spirit was given, he offered them money, saying, 'Give me this power also, that anyone on whom I lay hands may receive the Holy Spirit.'" When the Samaritans received the Holy Spirit, a physical reaction was present because Simon, the sorcerer, saw that through the laying on of the apostle's

hands, the Holy Spirit was given. Notice, also Acts 19:6, which says, "And when Paul had laid hands on them, the Holy Spirit came upon them, and they spoke with tongues and prophesied." Please notice there was another physical reaction; they spoke with tongues. Now, if the Scriptures just said, "they spoke" then there would have been no need for any mention of it. The Scriptures does mention that they spoke with Tongues. This "Tongues" if it were of normal speech would carry no significant value whatsoever, especially one, noteworthy of Scripture. This "Tongues" however, appeared so different and was so strange that it carried enough significance, or it was noteworthy enough to be mentioned prominently in this Scriptural account.

B. The tongues spoken on Pentecost were no doubt used of the Lord to attract the interests of the "devout men, out of every nation under heaven," that were at Jerusalem at that time (Acts 2:5). This we see as part of the historical record given to us in the Scriptures, but we do not agree, with the expositors who regard the Pentecostal outpouring as the Lord's way of attracting a multitude of men from around the world. Our reason for this belief is that, in later instances recorded in the Scriptures, we find tongues being given without a multitude of people being present. Please refer to these scriptures: Acts 10:1-46, only Cornelius's household; Acts 19:1-7, only about 12 were baptized, refer to 1 Corinthians 12-14.

Now let us look at what the purpose of speaking in an unknown tongue as the Spirit gives utterance is.

1. It is for men to speak supernaturally to God.
   Every consecrated believer must have felt at times a consuming desire to open his heart to God in unspeakable communication and adoration with words that cannot be uttered. That depth of love can only find its expression as

Spirit anointed words of heavenly praise burst forth from our innermost being—Yes, even from the Holy Spirit Himself, who speaks directly to God mysteries too marvelous for us to comprehend in our own finite minds. Have you never wept because of how helpless your words are to express emotion in the presence of Him whom your soul loves? This marvelous Gift of Tongues will give you the words and expressions needed because they come from only the Spirit of God that dwells inside you. Notice 1 Corinthians 14:2, "For he who speaks in a tongue does not speak to men but to God, for no one understands him; however, in the spirit he speaks mysteries."

2. It is for every believer's help in praying more effectively.
Have you ever in the presence of Jesus felt inarticulate when prayer is so badly needed and the problem to immense to articulate properly, or felt so weak under the load of Satan's attacks, that the words were just not available? Look at Romans 8:26, "Likewise the Spirit also helps in our weaknesses. For we do not know what we should pray for as we ought, but the Spirit Himself makes intercession for us with groanings which cannot be uttered."

3. It is for believers so they can magnify God.
In the house of Cornelius at Caesarea, the new converts "spoke with tongues and magnified God" (Acts 10:46). What glory there would be if all Christians spoke with tongues! What a great magnification it would also bring to the Lord who is so worthy of all our praise, honor, and glory. Does He not deserve all the praise, honor, and glory we can give Him? Cornelius's household magnified God. They exalted God's greatness as they broke into the Spirit's rapturous expressions. There are no terms in natural speech appropriate to express God's greatness, only in supernatural speech can we even attempt to come close to giving Him the praise, honor, glory and majesty that He deserves as the King of Kings and the Lord of Lords, the Lamb slain

before the foundation of the world. How great is our God! How great is His name!

4. It is to help edify ourselves.
1 Corinthians 14:4 says, "He who speaks in a tongue edifies himself, but he who prophesies edifies the church." You may edify (building up, promotion of spiritual growth) others by teaching, preaching, or prophesying. With tongues however, we edify ourselves. Who is there among us who does not need to be built up or promoted to spiritual growth? Speaking to God in the Spirit edifies us. Being filled with the Spirit and yielding to the sweet exercise of speaking or singing with other tongues (refer Ephesians 5:19) builds ourselves up, and magnifies the Lord at the same time, while making melody to Him in our hearts (1 Corinthians 14:15).

5. It is to make our prayer life much more effective.
1 Corinthians 14:14, "For if I pray in a tongue, my spirit prays, but my understanding is unfruitful." Notice you are praying in a tongue and your understanding is unfruitful. In other words, you do not know what you are praying for, all you know is by faith you are praying words of edification to yourself and magnifying God at the same time. The only way to pray with the Spirit is to pray in tongues that are anointed and inspired by the Spirit Himself. Do you pray with your spirit or with your understanding? I hope both. Praying with the Spirit is quite different from praying with the understanding (verse 16). While praying with your understandings is extremely important, praying in tongues, or allowing the Holy Spirit to pray through you is also extremely valuable. When we pray with our understanding, we pray for the things which we know to be important and needed for ourselves and others. However, our prayers are limited because our understanding is limited. They can also be misdirected due to sin, such as selfish desires, pride, greed, loneliness, and so on. However, when the Holy Spirit of God is praying through us, there is no sin, desire, or lack of understanding that can limit or hinder the prayer. God

is then praying, and He knows what is best and the most beneficial for us, our situation, and the world. What better way is there then to allow the God of the universe to ask Himself to make changes in us and in the world?

6. It is a gift from the Father in heaven.

Jesus told His disciples in John 14:16-17, "And I will pray the Father, (all biblical references to the Son, Father or Holy Spirit are capitalized refer to the NKJV for references) and He will give you another Helper, that He may abide with you forever—the Spirit of truth, whom the world cannot receive, because it neither sees Him nor knows Him; but you know Him, for He dwells with you and will be in you". Also, in John 14:25-27, "These things I have spoken to you while being present with you. But the Helper, the Holy Spirit. whom the Father will send in My name. He will teach you all things, and bring to your remembrance all things that I said to you. And you also will bear witness, because you have been with me from the beginning".

The apostle Paul speaking to the Corinthian church asked, "Or do you not know that your body is the temple of the Holy Spirit who is in you, whom you have from God, and you are not your own? For you were bought at a price; therefore, glorify God in your body and in your spirit, which are God's" (1 Corinthians 6:19-20, emphasis added). God in you [is] the hope of glory (Colossians 1:27).

We have now examined what the different aspects of why the Holy Spirit was given to man, sometimes however, it is extremely valuable when investigating something to investigate what something is not for even better understanding. Understanding what something is not often helps in understanding what the something actually is. I believe that this is one of those times.

1. "Tongues" is not human languages given to accelerate the spread of the Gospel.

This theory simply states that speaking with tongues in the early church was the supernatural communication of the Gospel in languages unknown to the speaker but known to the hearers. This is perhaps the oldest and most widely known theory. Its proponents say that without the Gift of Tongues, the disciples would have been faced with the task of mastering many languages before they could witness to the uttermost parts of the earth. Therefore, at Pentecost God gave them the ability to preach the Gospel in a multitude of human languages they had never learned, so the Good News (Gospel) could be spread quickly all over the world.

Though it is absolutely true that at Pentecost foreign languages were spoken by the 120 and understood by the bystanders, and it is equally true that this phenomenon has been repeated in many and varied circumstances since that day. For example, Stanley Howard Frodsham, in his book With Signs Following, has given a series of testimonies, which illustrate the fact that speaking with tongues has been used of God to acquaint foreigners with the Gospel in a supernatural and spectacular manner. Nevertheless, the objection comes when they say that this was the primary or only use of tongues in the early church. It is in my opinion the speaking in foreign languages on the day of Pentecost was the exception and not the rule.

When one reads the text closely, he finds that only the 120 were so endued with this power from on high. They continued to magnify God for quite a while, for it took time for the crowd of over 3,000 to arrive. The record of Acts 2 does not imply that any outsiders were present when the disciples began to speak in those unlearned languages. Only that these amazed spectators came because they overheard the pure worship of the 120 declaring the wonderful works of God. Now I ask you, does the scripture tell us that they were speaking in tongues because the crowd gathered or did the crowd gather because they were speaking with tongues? The scripture tells us that it was the latter. Also, no preaching was done by the 120 until after the crowd arrived.

This is the problem with this theory. The only preaching done on the day of Pentecost was by Peter after the miracle of tongues took place. Peter, "standing up with the eleven, raised his voice and said to them, 'Men of Judea and all who dwell in Jerusalem, let this be known to you, and heed my words' (Acts 2:14). How could all these men of different tongues have anything made known to them or hearken to Peter's words unless they all knew what Peter was saying? Or was it that Peter was speaking in a foreign language and they were hearing it in their own languages, making the miraculous sign of tongues one of hearing not of speaking?

When one examines closely the text of Acts 2 it becomes easy to understand that at Pentecost "tongues" was not needed for a clear comprehension of the Gospel. Hearing their native tongues spoken by the Galileans astonished the multitude, that astonishment forced them to gather together to see what was happening. Then Peter preached. It was Peter's message, in a language known by all, anointed by God, and filled with the saving Grace of the Holy Spirit which conveyed the Gospel to them. Three thousand people received salvation through Peter's message. Oh, God, give us this level of anointing and power, in order to reach this lost and dying world with exactly the same effect. Amen!

Finally, there is not the slightest implication anywhere in Scripture that the Apostles ever employed tongues as a means of preaching the Gospel to foreigners. Paul makes it very clear in 1st Corinthians 14 that when he was teaching or preaching, he never employed the Gift of Tongues. In fact, he spoke against using it for that purpose (1 Corinthians 14:6).

2. "Tongues" is not utterances of the subconscious mind.

If it were true that the speaking with other tongues at Pentecost was a result of abnormally quickened memories springing forth from one's subconscious mind, it might follow that a similar reason can be offered for other types of supernatural utterances in the Bible. Consider, for example the case of the tower at Babel (Genesis 11:6-9). Perhaps a still more amazing miracle of the talking donkey (Numbers 22:28-30). Surely, the rationalist is in for a difficult time if they attempt to convince us that these words sprang from the subconscious mind of the donkey.

3. It is not an accelerated ability to learn foreign languages.

Paul plainly shows that "if I pray in an unknown tongue my Spirit prays, but my understanding is unfruitful" (1 Corinthians 14:14, KJV,) How can we speak in an unknown tongue if we have already learned the tongue?

4. It is not only the ability to speak in foreign languages never before learned.

This idea states that on the day of Pentecost, the 120 in the upper room were filled with the Holy Ghost, and began to speak in foreign languages. Therefore, all subsequent infillings with the evidence of speaking in other tongues were of the exact same nature. When asked for a specific reason for this the proponents of this theory say that it was to help the disciples of Christ in the quick spreading of the Gospel worldwide (refer to number one).

All the men present, that witnessed the miracle of the baptism of the Holy Spirit with the evidence of speaking in other tongues, were men that came from foreign countries where there was a large Jewish population. The Judean and Galilean dialects of Aramaic were readily spoken by all. There was no need therefore, for the men speaking in an unknown tongue to speak in foreign languages so the Gospel could be quickly spread throughout the world.

But even with this argument, the doctrinal error persists. Why? Because just a general reading of the account of Acts 2:1-11, especially verses 6 and 11 leaves one with the idea that this could possibly be true. However, when we look in the Word of God and study to show ourselves approved unto God, rightly dividing the Word of truth (2 Timothy 2:15), we see some interesting information that helps us see that the idea that on the day of Pentecost the 120 in the upper room began to speak in foreign languages, and therefore, all subsequent infillings were of the exact nature, cannot be the case.

For example, in 1 Corinthians 14:2 (KJV), we read, "For he that speaks in an unknown tongue speaks not unto men, but unto God: for no man understands him; howbeit in the spirit he speaks mysteries" (Emphasis added). If God created all languages, how then, if we are speaking in foreign languages does no one understand? Is a mystery something that is known? Doesn't the word no man include you? Remember, 1 Corinthians 14:14 (KJV), "If I pray in an unknown tongue my Spirit prays, but my understanding is unfruitful?" (Emphasis added). What about 1 Corinthians 13:1, "Though I speak with the tongues of men and of angels" (Emphasis added). What exactly are the tongues of angels, Latin maybe? How about French, Italian, or maybe Swahili? Or could it be exactly what Paul calls it, "an unknown tongue."

These verses together show that the Holy Spirit's tongue or language is totally different and distinct from anything we have learned on earth. It is a language that only God understands. It is a personal intimate language that God gave us to glorify and magnify Himself (Acts 10:46).

What about Acts 2:1-11? Were they not speaking in foreign languages? Do not verses 6 and 11 leave us with that exact impression? Then the question why the different languages? How do we explain this seemingly obvious statement made in verses 6 and 11 that "every man heard them speak in his own language" and "we do hear them speaking in our tongues?"

I present to you two explanations. The first being they did speak in foreign languages unknown to them at the time of the infilling, but it was not for the quick spreading of the Gospel specifically as a result of preaching in these different languages, but rather this miracle was used for the attracting of the crowd in order for the Gospel to be spread. There are many incidences in scripture that point to miracles attracting people so that the Gospel can be heard (Ref. Matthew 11:3-5; Luke 23:8; John 2:11, 23; 3:2; 6:2,14; 7:31;12:18; Acts 14:8-15; etc.). Even today, miracles, and healing crusades are advertised for the same reason, they attract attention, attention draws crowds, and many come to know Christ.

D.A. Hayes cites a modern manifestation of tongues which appears to be somewhat similar to this Pentecostal experience, he recalls that,

> During the Welsh revival of 1904, young Welshmen and Welshwomen who could not speak a dozen words in Welsh in ordinary conversation were remarkably and, as it seemed to them, supernaturally empowered to pray fervently and fluently for five or ten minutes in idiomatic Welsh. This enabling to speak, in what was supposedly an unknown tongue, was to many people the most remarkable feature of that most remarkable revival.[9]

Also consider that they might not be speaking in foreign languages but different dialects they had never learned before. Please notice Acts 2:7; it says that all the men who spoke with tongues were Galileans. The Galileans, as well as, the Judeans spoke the very same language in Christ's day, Aramaic. Aramaic is called Hebrew in the New Testament.

After the exile, the Aramaic language gradually became the popular language of Palestine, not only of Galilee and Samaria, but also of Judea. Christ and the apostles spoke it." So, an explanation must be offered for the astonishment which the Judeans manifested when they heard the Galileans speaking in the Judean tongue. This fact most certainly suggests a linguistic difference of some kind.[10]

Matthew Henry's comments will also help shine some light on this difficult passage,

Thence we come in order to Judea, which ought to be mentioned, because though the language was the same with that which the disciples spoke, yet before, they spoke it with a north country tone and dialect, "thou art a Galilean, and thy speech betrayed thee" (Matthew 26:73), but now they spoke it as correctly as the inhabitants of Judea themselves did. This speaking without an accent and this forming of a number of strictly Judean words was as impossible to the Galileans as it was for the Ephraimites to say, "Shibboleth" (Judges 12:6). It was as miraculous for their north country tone and dialect no longer to betray them, as it was for their other glossolalic brethren to speak pure Latin, or Persian, or Arabic.[11]

Whatever you believe about the miracle of Acts 2 and what the foreign languages actually were, keep it within the context of your understanding of these two very important facts.

1. The miracle was not and cannot be made the rule for all further infillings.

2. Tongues was not needed for the rapid spread of the Gospel.

Scripture is categorically opposed to these ideas.
Before we close this chapter, a word of exhortation is necessary.

First: *A Word to the Unsaved.* If you are among that number, we would urge you to delay no longer in becoming acquainted with Jesus. Will you not, this moment, fly to the bosom of Him who loved you enough to die for you, that you might be forgiven for your sin? For the wages of sin is eternal death. Will you not enter now into the presence of Him, who can save you from the guilt and power of sin and who can bring a deep, settled peace into your soul? Will you not this day surrender your all to Him who surrendered His all for you? Do it now! You will never regret it, A former pastor's wife of mine, a very wise woman, once said, "no matter where you are on the ladder of success, God can always take you to the next step upward." God told us to test Him and know that He is God. Will you take a step of faith today? Test God! He will bring you higher than you have ever been before.

Second: *A Word to Non-Pentecostal Christians.* You have an opportunity now to examine in depth the Pentecostal view of speaking with other tongues. However, we would remind each of you that the reading of this study means that you must ultimately make a decision, either to accept the facts contained herein or to reject the facts regarding the blessed Gift of God we call "Speaking with other Tongues." Even though you must decide, we would not encourage you to make a hasty decision, for the cost of your decision is extremely high. If you accept our belief concerning tongues, you face the possible loss of your religious reputation, ecclesiastical position, lifelong friendships, and even temporal comforts. On the other hand, if you reject it, you will be rejecting that which an overwhelming amount of evidence proclaims as truth and the spiritual heights that can only be obtained by the infilling of the Holy Spirit in His fullness. Brethren, we beseech you to count the cost carefully and prayerfully. Ask God for grace to suffer the loss of all things rather than to sacrifice this priceless Gift.

Third: *A Word to Pentecostal Christians.* It is our sincere hope that this study has strengthened your belief in the Scriptural perfection of the Pentecostal experience of the baptism in the Holy Spirit, with the evidence of speaking with other tongues. We would do well to remember that this blessed privilege also brings a solemn responsibility. The baptism of the Holy Spirit, with the initial evidence of speaking with other tongues was given for a specific purpose. That purpose is to give us power to be witnesses for Christ. Acts 1:8 says, "But you shall receive power when the Holy Spirit has come upon you; and you shall be witnesses to Me in Jerusalem, and in all Judea and Samaria, and to the end of the earth." We must walk in the light that God has graciously shed upon our pathway. We must witness to the world around us as children bent on one purpose and one purpose alone. That purpose is to bring the Gospel of peace to the unsaved with all the zeal the knowledge of Christ's soon coming and the eternal punishment for all who do not know him brings to our hearts. This solemn responsibility can only be accomplished "not by might, nor by power, but by My Spirit, saith the Lord of hosts" (Zechariah.4:6 KJV). Therefore, brethren, let us pray for a constant, personal strengthening of might by His Spirit in the inner man and for a new outpouring of His Spirit upon the entire Church in these last days.

Chapter Questions To Help Your Study

1. The baptism with the Holy Spirit, according to the late Dr. R. A. Torrey is three things, what are they?
2. Tongues is; the initial, physical evidence of the baptism of the Holy Spirit. True or False
3. Give two different aspects in regard to Baptism in the Holy Spirit with the evidence of speaking in tongues?
4. Give four different purposes for speaking in an unknown tongue as the Spirit gives utterance.
5. Give three things tongues are not.
6. The Baptism of the Holy Spirit was given for a specific purpose, what is that purpose?
7. The solemn responsibility of witnessing can only be accomplished.
8. There is a simple classification of Spiritual Gifts. They fall naturally into three groups. What are those groups?

THE CLASSIFICATION AND MOTIVATION OF SPIRITUAL GIFTS

I n order to accurately classify and study the Spiritual Gifts we must put them in their proper perspective. We can only do this by taking special notice of the central premise in which all the Spiritual Gifts are given. That central premise can be found in 1 Corinthians 12:7 KJV. "But the manifestation of the Spirit is given to every man to profit withal".

The Spirit of God is manifest by exercising these Gifts. They show us that God is in our midst, and He is able and willing to help His children. These Gifts are a trust put into the hands of specific brethren, to profit everyone, not for the honor, prestige, and benefit of those who they are given. They are specifically intended for the benefit of the entire "Body of Christ," and to spread the Gospel throughout the world. The more one uses them to bestow profit on others, the more abundantly they will be blessed (Philippians 4:7).

With this in mind, let us now classify the Spiritual Gifts in order to make them easier to study. In 1 Corinthians 12:8-11, Paul said, "...for to one is given the word of wisdom through the Spirit, to another the word of knowledge through the same Spirit, to another faith by the same Spirit, to another gifts of healings by the same Spirit, to another the working of miracles, to another prophecy, to another discerning of spirits, to another different kinds of tongues, to another the interpretation of tongues. But one and the same Spirit works all these things, distributing to each one individually as He wills."

The Gifts mentioned in the above passage fall naturally into three groups, with each of these groups containing three Gifts. There are three Gifts of Revelation, three Gifts of Power, and three Gifts of Inspiration. The fourth group of Spiritual Gifts that will be examined is found in Ephesians 4:11; this verse contains what are called the five Administrative Gifts.

The list or group classifications found below were taken from Harold Horton's book, The Gifts of the Spirit. Obviously, they do not follow the same order as the Gifts in the above passage. Even though these groupings or classifications appear nowhere in scripture, if we set them up in this easy to read format, it will help us when referring to them.

1. Gifts of Revelation:
   A. A Word of Wisdom—A supernatural revelation of future facts set forth for a divine purpose.
   B. A Word of Knowledge—A supernatural revelation of present or past facts set forth for a divine purpose.
   C. Discerning of Spirits—A supernatural insight into the realm of the spirit. This insight allows the discerner to recognize the operation of spirits, both good and evil.

2. Gifts of Power:
   A. Faith—A supernatural power to believe (passive) in God for the miraculous.
   B. The Working of Miracles—A super natural intervention (active) in the ordinary and natural course of nature.
   C. Gifts of Healing—A supernatural power to heal diseases (active) beyond the ordinary ability and course of human recuperative powers.

3. Gifts of Inspiration (Vocal Gifts):

    A. Prophecy—A supernatural comment in a known tongue.

    B. Divers Kinds of Tongues—A supernatural utterance in an unknown tongue.

    C. Interpretation of Tongues—A supernatural explanation of the meaning of the unknown tongues.

4. Gifts of Administration:

    A. Apostles—one supernaturally empowered and sent forth with the ability to establish, oversee, and direct many parts of the body of Christ.

    B. Prophets one supernaturally empowered to speak forth God's divine message of instruction and direction.

    C. Evangelists—a supernatural messenger of God that spreads the Good News of the Gospel and proclaims the glad tidings of salvation. Many Missionaries are essentially evangelists.

    D. Pastors—one supernaturally empowered to tend the flock of God. Not merely to feed but also to guide and protect.

    E. Teachers—one supernaturally empowered to instruct God's people in the truth of the entire Gospel of Christ.

These Gifts can be categorized in other formats as well. One such format is as follows. There are three persons of the Godhead, Father, Son, and Holy Spirit. Each specific individual has given us specific Gifts.

1. The Father—gave us what is referred to as the Motivational Gifts": Prophecy, Mercy, Giving, Teaching, Exhortation, Serving, and Administrations (Ref. Romans 12:6-8).

2. The Son—gave us what is referred to as the "Five-Fold Ministry Gifts": Apostles, Prophets, Evangelists, Pastors and Teachers (Refer Ephesians 4:11)

3. The Holy Spirit—gave us what is referred to as the "Gifts of the Holy Spirit:" the Word of Wisdom, Word

of Knowledge, Discerning of Spirits, Faith, Working of Miracles, Gifts of healings, Prophecy, Different kinds of tongues, Interpretation of tongues (Refer 1 Corinthians 12:7–11).

This writer sees nothing wrong with this categorization. Seeing that the Father, Son, and Holy Spirit are all one in person, and purpose, this method of categorization changes nothing. Therefore, for the purpose of this book we will use Harold Horton's format. One benefit of this other categorization is the difficulty it presents to those who do not believe that the Gifts are for today. For, if each individual of the Godhead brings His own set of Spiritual Gifts then to deny any of the Gifts is to deny the presence and existence of its Giver in modern times. Seeing that no man who calls himself "Christian" would deny the existence of any member of the Godhead the denial of any Gift then becomes impossible.

Please notice that we have utilized the words "supernatural" or "supernaturally" in the definition of every one of the Gifts of the Spirit. This is because the Gifts are miraculous. Man's ability or abilities are in no way being utilized when these Gifts are in operation. Each Gift goes beyond, and is independent of, any knowledge or ability man possesses. Man is only the vessel God chooses to operate through, exactly in the same way as a car operating under the direction of a driver. Also, notice the order in which the Gifts appear in 1 Corinthians 12:8-11. It has been suggested by Harold Horton that these three groups overflow and interlock.

There are two revelation Gifts and one power Gift, then two power Gifts and one inspiration Gift, and finally, one revelation Gift and two inspiration Gifts, from which we might learn that God's infinities cannot be divided. His omnipotence is not separate from His omniscience. They are co-equal and co-active. We can isolate them, so to speak, for the purposes of analysis and examination, like the individual colors of the spectrum: but they are not separate because they are distinct. They merge, harmonize and flow with one another, and who shall say where one begins and the other ends. By the Gifts of the Spirit man gets an experience, at the will of the Spirit, of God's infinite knowledge, ability, and even His infinite presence.[12]

It has been suggested by some truly esteemed Christian brethren, that the Gifts of the Spirit are optional; you can live a godly life without them. I agree! But the godly life, in which you would be living, however, would be limited in insight, power, and the God given ability to make directed and specific changes in all situations. The Gifts of the Spirit give you the ability to act instead of react. If you could see a wall before hitting it, is it not better? In other words, Spiritual Gifts are as optional as eyesight; you can walk without eyes, but you cannot see without them. You can live a godly life without the Gifts of the Spirit, but you cannot be mighty in God without them. Desiring only to live a godly life alone is at best self-centered and self-gratifying. To be mighty in God, and in so doing change the world around us, is self-sacrificing and godly exaltation. God is looking for people after His own heart, people who will live a self-sacrificing life.

Spiritual Gifts are about being powerful in God, and power is what the Gifts supply. Living a godly life is only one part of a Christian's life, living powerfully is another! Brethren we are not only to be changed, but also to change the world around us. This can only effectively happen by the use of the Spiritual Gifts. If one desires to live godly, he must be obedient. If it is true that living godly consists, and can only exist in obedience, then as children of the most high, we must also obey the command to "desire spiritual gifts" (1 Corinthians 14:1).

The possession and use of Spiritual Gifts in believers are an absolute necessity to Christ, because "as the body is one, and hath many members...so also is Christ" (1 Corinthians 12:12, KJV). The apostle Paul tells us in 1 Corinthians 12:12-31, that they are as natural to God in the carrying out of His present purposes as our arms, legs, hands, and feet. These verses state as clearly as anything could that, so far as a ministry of miraculous power is concerned, the body of Christ, without the Gifts of the Spirit, is like a body without arms, legs, eyes, ears, etc.

The Gifts of the Spirit operating through God's children are like divine senses and/or appendages to the Lord. We are His children and members of His Body. He chooses to use His children. The Gifts are as eyes, ears, feet, lips, and hands to Him. "As He is, so are we in this world" (1 John 4:17). We, as children of God, must ask ourselves, Would we be better off trying to find our way through this evil world, by the use of a cane, or like a blind man who gropes about not knowing what is about to befall him, or with fully functioning senses, which are empowered by God, seeing pitfalls ahead, and knowing exactly where the Spirit of God is leading? How much help is a blind man who is groping about not knowing where he is going, to those in need of insight and direction? Jesus referring to this exact situation said, "Let them alone. They are blind leaders of the blind. And if the blind leads the blind, both will fall into a ditch" (Matthew 15:14). If we are God's ambassadors with a ministry of reconciliation (2 Corinthians 5:18-20), how can we do our jobs if we are blind leaders of the blind? In order to prevent the calamity of falling into a ditch, Jesus left us with the precious Gifts of the Spirit. In order to be ambassadors of Christ and to fulfill the ministry of reconciliation these Gifts of the Spirit are essential. If we are trying to minister, without using His divine senses, we are nothing more than blind leaders of the blind whose end is death.

Now, let's examine what the purpose and end result of these supernatural Gifts of the Spirit are. Let's start by reading 1 Corinthians 12:12-27;

For as the body is one, and has many members, but all the members of that one body, being many, are one body, so also is Christ. For by one Spirit we were all baptized into one body, whether Jews or Greeks, whether slaves or free and have all been made to drink into one Spirit. For in fact the body is not one member but many. If the foot should say, "Because I am not a hand, I am not of the body," is it therefore not of the body? And if the ear should say, "Because I am not an eye, I am not of the body," is it therefore not of the body? If the whole body were an eye, where would be the hearing? If the whole were hearing, where would be the smelling? But now God has set the members, each one of them, in the body just as He pleased. And if they were all one member, where would the body be? But now indeed there are many members, yet one body. And the eye cannot say to the hand, "I have no need of you"; or again the head to the feet, "I have no need of you." No, much rather, those members of the body which seem to be weaker are necessary. And those members of the body which we think to be less honorable, on these we bestow greater honor; and our unpresentable parts have greater modesty, but our presentable parts have no need. But God composed the body, having given greater honor to that part which lacks it, that there should be no schism in the body, but that the members should have the same care for one another. And if one member suffers, all the members suffer with it; or if one member is honored, all the members rejoice with it. Now you are the body of Christ, and members individually.

Notice these phrases; the body is one, by one spirit, made to drink into one Spirit, yet but one body. The same message appears in the opening verses of Ephesians 4, where the Administrative Gifts of the Spirit are found.

> "I, therefore, the prisoner of the Lord, beseech you to walk worthy of the calling with which you were called, with all lowliness and gentleness, with longsuffering, bearing with one another in love, endeavoring to keep the unity of the Spirit in the bond of peace. There is one body and one Spirit, just as you were called in one hope of your calling; one Lord, one faith, one baptism; one God and Father of all, who is above all, and through all, and in you all."
>
> Ephesians 4:1-6

The emphasis in these two passages is clearly on the recurrent word one. The word one appears thirteen times in the seventeen verses of 1 Corinthians 12., and eight times in the opening six verses of Ephesians 4,

The lesson emphasized in these passages is extremely simple to understand. Spiritual Gifts emanate from only one source; they should be manifested in oneness; and should produce oneness in those who possess them. But what is the ultimate purpose? The ultimate purpose is so that God's children can come into the fullness of Christ. Because, cooperation and unity inspire men to improve their conditions (2 Kings 6:1-3), it encourages reform (1 Chronicles 12:38), and it helps in the carrying out of great and mighty works for God (Nehemiah 4:16-17). Cooperation also gives added power in prayer (Matthew 18:19), in Spiritual Warfare (Deuteronomy 32:30, Mark 6:7), and it helps to bring men to Christ (Mark 2:3). Cooperation and unity makes us an unbeatable army (Judges 6), one much more capable of succeeding at any task that is set before

51

us (Genesis 11:6). Cooperation is essential to success (Nehemiah 4); it sustains us in times of weakness (Exodus 17:12), it gives boldness for battle (1 Samuel 14:6), and gives victory in battle (Judges 20:11).

We are a formidable force when we are walking together in unity and working together as one, just like a herd of Alaskan Elk being attacked by hungry wolves, gathers together in circled groups, all facing outward with their weapons (horns) at the ready. They can then effectively fend off the predators who are seeking their lives and the lives of the herd. In unity, we do the same. In the same way as an elk left alone against an advancing hoard of ravenous wolves will surely be easy prey, and his life expectancy short, so will it be with us if we are left alone against the wiles of our enemy, the devil. "For he is like a roaring lion seeking whom he may devour" (I Peter 5:8). Without unity and cooperation, we are exactly like the lone elk facing the hoard of ravenous wolves. We die!

Thus far, we have seen the importance of unity and cooperation, but how long shall we remain unified? "Till we all come to the unity of the faith and of the knowledge of the Son of God, to a perfect man, to the measure of the stature of the fullness of Christ" (Ephesians 4:13). Why? So "that we should no longer be children, tossed to and fro and carried about with every wind of doctrine, by the trickery of men, in the cunning craftiness of deceitful plotting" (Ephesians 4:14). How will this be accomplished? By "speaking the truth in love, [that we] may grow up in all things into Him who is the head – Christ, from whom the whole body, joined and knit together by what every joint supplies, according to the effective working by which every part does its share, causes growth of the body for the edifying of itself in love" (Ephesians 4:15-16).

The lesson of 1 Corinthians 12 along with its message of unity also includes a warning against schisms resulting from envy and competition in the use of the Gifts of the Spirit. "And those members of the body which we think to be less honorable, on these we bestow greater honor; and our unpresentable parts have greater modesty, but our presentable parts have no need. But God composed the body having given greater honor to that part which lacks it, that there should be no schism in the body, but that the members should have the same care for one another" 1 Corinthians 12:23-25, The problem of schisms, envy, lust, and pride was; not unusual in the Corinth church. As we examine the Corinthian Epistles, we see this same problem reoccurring again and again. Examine, if you please 1 Corinthians 1:10-31, 3:1-8, 6:1-6, 6:9-20, 12:23-25. These sections of Scripture show why Paul stressed "the message of unity based on the foundation of love: in 1 Corinthians 13; more on that in a moment.

But for now, let me point out a false teaching circulating in modern Christianity concerning the meaning of the phrase, "… earnestly desire the best gifts" (1 Corinthians 12:31, emphasis added). Many in Christendom believe that this instruction means that we are not to seek the Gifts of the Spirit, but to seek only the best gift, love. This instruction is totally in error! 1 Corinthians 14:1 categorically affirms that there is a difference between love and Spiritual Gifts and instructs us to seek after both.

Although Paul suggests in 1 Corinthians 12:31, that there are different levels of greatness in the Gifts and that we should "… earnestly desire the best gifts" (plural), he goes on to say "and yet I show you a more excellent way." Notice please the word "way," it is not the word "gifts." Paul never suggests that we seek only love. If we are to believe as our misguided brethren do, then we must answer the question of why. Why did Paul, after instructing us on the benefits, and use of a long list of Spiritual Gifts decide to tell us not to seek those Gifts, but to seek only love, which our misguided brethren believe is the best gift (singular)?

It is at this point that I would like to clarify a misnomer. The Bible never calls love a Gift of the Spirit. Love is a Fruit of the Spirit (Galatians 5:22). Love is the very nature of God (1 John 4:8). When we hear someone referring to the "gift of love," they are referring to the grace of love, which brought us benefits and blessings beyond our imagination. Graces such as salvation, eternal life, mercy, peace, communion with God, adoption, etc., not love itself. We receive His love when we ask God into our hearts for again, God's very nature is love (1 John 4: 8).

Paul's meaning in 1 Corinthians 12:31 is simply to earnestly desire the most useful and excellent Gifts, the most beneficial and edifying Gifts, such as are most advantageous to the Church (refer 1 Corinthians 14:12). The church in Corinth, as stated earlier, was filled with schisms resulting from envy and competition in the use of the Gifts of the Spirit. Paul, knowing this, says he will show us a more excellent way, specifically referring to the grace of love. The sanctifying graces of the Holy Spirit are more excellent than the miraculous. Charity, or love toward God and our neighbor, surpasses the best of gifts, even though the gifts are very extraordinary, supernatural, and miraculous. Therefore, it is the Christian's duty to be more covetous and desirous of them, for when the Gifts vanish away (1 Corinthians 13:8), the behavior of grace shall never fail, but abide forever. Paul is telling us that there is a greater excellence in grace, particularly those graces found in the Love of God.

When Jesus was asked what the greatest commandment was, He responded with two commands of action. "Thou shalt love the Lord thy God with all thy heart, and with all thy soul, and with all thy mind. This is the first and great commandment. And the second is like unto it, "thou shalt love thy neighbor as thyself." On these two commandments hang all the law and the prophets" (Matthew 22:35-40 KJV). Please notice that both these commands are demonstrations of love—loving God and loving man. These actions are called the greatest two commandments. This plainly shows that love is the more excellent way and the graces resulting from love are the best of all gifts.

One last note, the texts for studying the Gifts of the Spirit are found mainly in Ephesians 4:11 and 1 Corinthians 12 and 14. Sandwiched between 1 Corinthians 12 and 14 is chapter 13, the "Love Chapter." One of the basic rules for proper Biblical interpretation is to understand that a text without a context is a pretext. In other words, 1 Corinthians 13 must be kept within the context of 1 Corinthians 12 and 14 if a proper interpretation is to be discovered.

Brethren, what I am about to say might come as a shock. 1 Corinthians 13 is not a dissertation on Love as a Gift. The subject of 1 Corinthians 13 is not even Love itself; although, it does contain a vivid and complete definition of love. Let me finish before you put this book down and start thinking that this writer has gone off the deep end. The subject of I Corinthians 13 is, Love as the motivation, power, and purpose for seeking and using Spiritual Gifts. 1 Corinthians 13 does not compare Spiritual Gifts and Love. It does not define Love as a Spiritual Gift. It compares Spiritual Gifts "without" Love and Spiritual Gifts "with" Love! It shows love as being the fuel that makes the Spiritual Gifts operate (verses 1-3).

Remember, we can only arrive at our ultimate destination by the narrow gate (Matthew 7:13). We can only find the narrow gate by the use of the Spiritual Gifts motivated, empowered, and driven by Love. The entire chapter of 1 Corinthians 13 deals with Spiritual Gifts empowered, controlled, and motivated by love. Just as all the fuel in the world without a map or the best map without any fuel will not enable us to get where we are going, it is the same with Spiritual Gifts without love or love without the Spiritual Gifts.

As stated earlier, 1 Corinthians 12 specifically deals with the Spiritual Gifts in regard to unity and edification in the Body of Christ. Why? Because schisms had developed in the Corinthian Church over which Gift was being used, who used them, how often they were being used, which was the greatest Gift, and so on. These schisms were obviously causing disunity and strife in the church. That is why 1 Corinthians 12:8-27 speaks about the Gifts in direct relation to unity in the body and the way the body works together as a unit. Now, with this in mind, it becomes clear what Paul was saying when he penned 1 Corinthians 12:31b, "And yet I show you a more excellent way" (emphasis added). A more excellent way to what? A more excellent way to seek and use the Spiritual Gifts. Don't seek or use them out of envy, lust, or pride but seek and use them in Agape love.

Any first year Bible student can tell you that the Bible originally did not have chapter and verse divisions. Each of the 66 books was originally written as documents or letters. They were compiled together to make up the book we now call the Bible. Therefore, although it is much simpler to read and study the Bible with the chapter and verse format, we should never forget that originally one sentence followed directly with another. With that said, let's look at 1 Corinthians 12:31 through 13:3.

> And yet I show you a more excellent way. (1 Corinthians 13:1) Though I speak with the tongues of men and of angels [notice the gift of tongues is in operation], but have not love [without Agape], I have become sounding brass or a clanging cymbal. (2) And though I have the gift of prophecy, and understand all mysteries and all knowledge, and though I have all faith, so that I could remove mountains [again the Gifts of the Spirit are in operation], but have not love [again without Agape], I am nothing. (3) And though I bestow all my goods to feed the poor, and though I give my body to be burned, but have not love, it profits me nothing."

Simply put, without love the Gifts of the. Spirit profit nothing!

Love, as the foundation and driving force of the Spiritual Gifts, turns them from a disadvantage into a tremendous advantage, from a weapon used by the enemy into a powerful, invincible weapon that can be used to destroy the works of the enemy. Most of all however, they can transform us from a wounded and defeated soldier into an invincible warrior who is more than a conqueror (Romans 8:37), through Christ who strengthens us (Philippians

4:13), so again Paul emphasizes that we should, "Pursue love, and desire spiritual gifts" (1 Corinthians 14:1a).

Is love the best way? Absolutely! Without love, the Spiritual Gifts are like magnificent, powerful horses that are unbridled and untamed all pulling in different directions. The result is the king's chariot goes nowhere fast. The chariot and its horses, as magnificent and beautiful as they are, become useless and ineffective for the journey ahead. But once these magnificent horses are harnessed to the King's chariot in love, with the reins secured and placed into the hands of the King of love, the chariot which carries the magnificence of the King of Kings will go forth in splendor, beauty, speed, and power, conquering all that stand before Him.

The Church of Jesus Christ is to be a hospital for the sick, a shelter in the time of storm, a home to the homeless, and a source of strength to the weak. It is a place of provision to the poor, a deliverance center to the oppressed, a place of life to the dead, and a preservative to the dying. The church is a place of faith to the faithless, hope to the hopeless, love to the unlovable. It is a place of knowledge to the unknowing, and a lighthouse to those who travel in darkness. It is a road map to the lost, food for the hungry, water for the thirsty, and comfort to the comfortless. It is security to those in fear, solid footing for them who are tossed to and fro. How then can the Church of Jesus Christ succeed without all God has provided for her use? She can only succeed by operating in the Gifts of the Spirit empowered, controlled, directed, and driven by the pure Agape love of God, the divine and driving force.

Chapter Questions To
Help Your Study

1. Each of these groups contains _gifts.
2. The fourth group can be found in Ephesians 4:11. They are referred to as the _____.
3. This group contains how many Gifts? List them.
4. Are we commanded to "desire the Spiritual Gifts"? Yes or No
5. What is the purpose and end result of these supernatural Gifts?

THE GIFTS THEMSELVES

N ow that the preparatory work has been done, we will start to examine the Gifts themselves. Before we start, however, let us first cover some important facts regarding ministry and the Gifts and then refresh our memories on some important facts about the Gifts of the Spirit. These facts, when completely understood, will give us greater understanding and appreciation for the Gifts themselves, a better command over their use, and a deeper faith in God, which will allow us to better serve the body of Christ and maintain our walk in Christ.

First, let me share a beautiful truth. Every Christian is called to ministry! Too often the clergy are seen as professional ministers and every aspect of ministry is theirs and theirs alone. The responsibility of the laity is restricted to going to church, singing and listening to messages often times designed to tickle one's ears. This notion is absolutely contrary to fundamental biblical teaching. The truth of the matter is that ministry is everyone's responsibility. My prayer is that this book will awaken the massive army of believers and cause them to be excited about ministry, and serve God to the best of their abilities.

What exactly is ministry anyway? It is the service of aiding others in the name of the Lord. This service or ministry (diakonos in the Greek) was used by Jesus when He said to His disciples, "... Whosoever will be great among you, let him be your minister [diakonos]" (Matthew 20:26). If we are to be Christians, which literately means Christ like, Jesus must be our example!

> Look not every man on his own things, but every
> man also on the things of others. Let this mind be
> in you, which was also in Christ Jesus: Who, being
> in the form of God, thought it not robbery to be
> equal with God: But made himself of no reputation,
> and took upon him the form of a servant, and was
> made in the likeness of men.
>
> Philippians 2:4-7

Our purpose for attending church has been distorted due to the lack of true biblical teaching in regard to the laity's and Church's true purpose. Too often our purpose is self-centered. We go to church because of habit, upbringing, a sense of morality, or when we are having a problem, or when we are going through troubles, or because we enjoy the ministry, pastor, music, the building, and even the sermons. The fact is, however, that the church is not for those things though they do help attendance. The purpose of the Church is not to be a social club or a good day out with the family; it is to be a training ground, a boot camp if you will, to prepare the army of God to fight a good fight, to stand against the wiles of the enemy, to be overcomers, to be salt and light to a lost and dying world. This world cannot afford only a few believers who do all the work while the majority of Christians sit and watch. If you need proof that this is true, just look around you. Is the Church changing the world or is the world changing the Church? It is the solemn task of Church leadership to train the army of God. They must train them to accomplish the task He has set before us. What is that task?

> "Go ye into all the world, and preach the gospel to
> every creature. He that believeth and is baptized
> shall be saved; but he that believeth not shall be
> damned. And these signs shall follow them that

believe; In my name shall they cast out devils; they shall speak with new tongues; They shall take up serpents; and if they drink any deadly thing, it shall not hurt them; they shall lay hands on the sick, and they shall recover."

Mark 16: 15-18

How many times does God have to give us the same command before we obey! Twice three times, how about five?! This commission is repeated at the end of every one of the Gospels and again in the first chapter of the book of Acts. Also, did you notice the use of the Gifts in this Great Commission? The mere mention of these Gifts in this Great Commission shows us their importance in regard to ministry and how vital it is not only to understand the importance of the Gifts of the Spirit, but to implement their use.

Now with that in mind let us go over these facts once again.

1. These Gifts are a trust put into the hands of specific brethren, to profit everyone, not for the honor, prestige, and benefit of those who they are given.
2. The Gifts belong to God and are freely given to every believer (1 Peter 4: 11).
3. The Gifts of the Spirit are given to every believer on the basis of faith, not works.
4. The main reasons that the Gifts of the Spirit are in such limited use in today's Church is unbelief, complacency, and fear.
5. Tongues, in regard to the Baptism of the Holy Spirit found in Acts 2, is distinct and separate from the Gift of tongues which is described in 1 Corinthians 12.
6. The Gifts can be easily categorized into four groups. The first three groups contain three Gifts and the fourth group contains five.

The four groups are:

A. Gifts of Revelation.
B. Gifts of Power.
C. Gifts of Inspiration.
D. Gifts of Administration.

7. The Gifts are supernatural; there is no element of the natural in any of them. They are all beyond and independent of any knowledge or ability of man.
8. These Gifts are for the glorification of the Father and the edification and unification of the saints. They will last until we all come to the unity of the faith and of the knowledge of the Son of God, to a perfect man, to the measure of the stature of the fullness of Christ; that we should no longer be children, tossed to and fro and carried about with every wind of doctrine, by the trickery of men...(Ephesians 4:13-14).
9. The Gifts of the Spirit are God's Gifts, for God to use, as God wills. They are to bring glory to God through the people God chooses to use. We are only the vessels God chooses to use, nothing more. All the Gifts God divides severally, as He wills, among various Christians. They should flow through the channels of the Christian's special and unique call into the common streams of public or church use. Then they ultimately return into the great ocean of His glory from whence they originally came, exactly like the way water vapor rises from the sea, meeting together in one cloud. That cloud then falls down divided into many distinct and separate drops. Those drops, when united, run together making streams of water, which when joined together run into brooks, those brooks turn into rivers and those rivers return to the sea from which it came. Thus, it is, with the Gifts of the Spirit.

THE GIFTS OF REVELATION

Revelation means to uncover or a drawing away of the veil of darkness, which covers the mystery and purpose of Christ. This revelation communicates the knowledge of God and the expression of God's will for man, for the specific purpose of instruction and guidance of the Church and its members.

A Word of Wisdom. From early in our Christian life, we were taught that God is Omniscient—He knows all things— and that God is Omnipresent—He is always there. in other words, God is not restricted by the dimension of space or time. He exists everywhere in the past, present, and future all at the same instant. Therefore, it stands to reason that if God exists in a dimension beyond the past, present, and future all at the same time; we can therefore understand that God is acutely aware of all facts in the past, present, and future.

This understanding constitutes His infinite Wisdom. Since God is ever conscious of all present things and future events, He must also be conscious of those present happenings that actually translate the present into the future. This divine understanding of what will happen in the future when any action is taken in the present is what we call God's foreknowledge. When God, who in His sovereign mercy, gives man a word or a glimpse of some event that has not yet happened, He is really giving man a revelation of His infinite protection, plan, and purpose. This is what we refer to as a Word of Wisdom.

The Word of Wisdom is a supernatural revelation by the Spirit of God concerning the divine purpose and plan of God that has not yet been realized by man. The Word of Wisdom always concerns future events. It is not a gift for unfolding God's revealed will, which is already written in His Word. It is for the unfolding of His unrevealed will and the declaration of His hidden purposes, apart from His Word. But it will never contradict what His written word has already revealed. It will however, give us a small glimpse into the future. It is therefore classified as a Gift of Revelation not of utterance.

Here are some biblical examples of how The Word of Wisdom was used.

1. Noah concerning future judgment. At God's command, Noah built an ark, one hundred and twenty years before God destroyed the earth in a universal flood (Genesis 6:13-18).
2. God informed Samuel concerning Saul's soon arrival, and Saul's appointment as king over Israel (1 Samuel 9:15-16). Also, Samuel's account of the events Saul would encounter as he returned home (1 Samuel 10:1-8).
3. God instructs Samuel to inform Saul about the kingdom being torn from him, due to his sin of disobedience (1 Samuel 15:10-29).
4. God sent Nathan the prophet to King David concerning the death of his unborn child, and the future events and ultimate downfall of his family, all as a result of David's sin with Bathsheba (2 Samuel 12:10-12).
5. Agabus the Prophet spoke to the church at Antioch concerning an upcoming famine (Acts 11:27-28).
6. Agabus the Prophet spoke to Paul concerning Paul's imprisonment in Jerusalem (Acts 21:10-11).
7. Paul received a word from God concerning the upcoming shipwreck and salvation of the crew (Acts 27:10-24).
8. Here is a modern-day example of a Word of Wisdom. Our family attended a small church in the Bronx, New York a number of years ago. In that church there was a blessed

sister in the Lord, who had a true relationship with Jesus. One day on her way home from work, the Lord spoke to this sister (we will call her Mary), and told her to walk home in a direction different than she had ever traveled before because danger waited. Mary questioned the Lord about the odd instruction. After all, she had been walking in this community and this same way home all her life. The only reply was, "walk home differently then you have previously." Doubt filled Mary's heart, and she did not obey; she felt that she misunderstood. She questioned within herself, why the Lord after so many years of walking home this particular way, would tell her to go home in another direction. Mary, filled with questions and doubts, disobeyed, and walked home in the same direction as usual. Crossing the street in front of her house, Mary was hit by a car. As a result of the accident, Mary had to have one of her feet from the ankle down amputated. Mary now walks with a prosthetic ankle and foot.

God, knowing the future because He is already there, warned Mary of an upcoming event that would keep His beloved child out of harm's way. Even though Mary disobeyed God's instruction, it does not change the fact that God, through a Word of Wisdom, revealed His foreknowledge of an upcoming dangerous and damaging event in Mary's life.

Take care at this point not to limit the definition of the Word of Wisdom. It is not exclusively for telling future events. It is however, God revealing His foreknowledge to man. This revelation of the foreknowledge of God is designed for protection, direction, instruction, or correction, not just information. Here are some examples of the different uses of the Word of Wisdom.

1. As shown above in the story of our sister Mary, it is to warn or guide God's people of future danger or judgment.
   A. As shown earlier Noah was warned of a flood that would destroy the world (Genesis 6).
   B. Lot was warned to escape Sodom due to the wrath of God, which would destroy Sodom and Gomorrah (Genesis 19).

2. The Word of Wisdom is used to reveal God's plan to those He is going to use.
   A. Joseph received a word from God to inform Pharaoh of the upcoming seven years of plenty and seven years of drought (Genesis 41). This Word of Wisdom resulted in Joseph being appointed as Pharaoh's second in charge of Egypt, and saved two nations at the same time.

3. A Word of Wisdom was used to assure a man of God of His divine call.
   A. Through the burning bush on Mount Horeb, God spoke to Moses telling Him that he was called to set God's people free (Exodus 3).

4. The Word of Wisdom is used to instruct God's people regarding places to go and people to see for effective witnessing.
   A. Peter was told by God to witness to the Gentiles. Go to a man's house by the name of Cornelius and witness (Acts 10).

5. The Word of Wisdom is used to reveal God's blessings and cursing, which are based directly on obedience or disobedience of His commands and ordinances.
   A. God gave His "Thou shalt" and "Thou shalt not" instructions to Moses and the children of Israel (Deuteronomy 28).

6. The Word of Wisdom is used to give assurance of future blessings.
   A. God spoke to Abraham that he was to inherit the land of Canaan (Genesis 12).
   B. God spoke to David that he was to inherit the throne of Israel (1 Samuel 16).

7. The Word of Wisdom is used to declare God's hidden mysteries.
   A. The entire book of Revelation is just such an example.

As marvelous and God ordained as the Word of Wisdom is, we must also recognize that the Word of Wisdom, as God reveals it, is not written in stone. The outcome can be changed. Here are some examples of how God's heart was changed, and so was the outcome of God's declaration.

1. Concerning the upcoming death of King Hezekiah (2 Kings 20:1-6).
   "In those days Hezekiah was sick and near death. And Isaiah the prophet, the son of Amos, went to him and said to him, "Thus says the LORD: `Set your house in order, for you shall die, and not live. Then he turned his face toward the wall, and prayed to the LORD, saying, remember now, O LORD, I pray, how I have walked before You in truth and with a loyal heart, and have done what was good in Your sight. "And Hezekiah wept bitterly. And it happened, before Isaiah had gone out into the middle court, that the word of the LORD came to him, saying, Return and tell Hezekiah the leader of My people, 'Thus says the LORD, the God of David your father "I have heard your prayer, I have seen your tears; surely I will heal you. On the third day you shall go up to the house of the LORD. And I will add to your days fifteen years. I will deliver you and this city from the hand of the king of Assyria; and I will defend this city for My own sake, and for the sake of My servant David."

In this passage, we see that Isaiah delivered God's message to Hezekiah the king. The message was that Hezekiah would soon die. Hezekiah immediately repented. God's heart was changed due to Hezekiah's repentance, and God sent Isaiah back to the King with the message that God heard his prayer. Because of Hezekiah's repentant heart, God changed his mind, giving King Hezekiah fifteen more years of life. If Hezekiah did not immediately repent, surely, he would have died within a few days.

2. Concerning Jonah, the Prophet and his message of destruction to the city of Nineveh (Jonah 1:2, 3:4-10). "Arise, go to Nineveh, that great city, and cry out against it; for their wickedness has come up before Me. And Jonah began to enter the city on the first day's walk. Then he cried out and said, "Yet forty days, and Nineveh shall be overthrown! So, the people of Nineveh believed God, proclaimed a fast, and put on sackcloth, from the greatest to the least of them. Then word came to the king of Nineveh; and he arose from his throne and laid aside his robe, covered himself with sackcloth and sat in ashes. And he caused it to be proclaimed and published throughout Nineveh by the decree of the king and his nobles, saying, let neither man nor beast, herd nor flock, taste anything; do not let them eat, or drink water. But let man and beast be covered with sackcloth, and cry mightily to God, yes, let everyone turn from his evil way and from the violence that is in his hands. Who can tell if God will turn and relent, and turn away from His fierce anger, so that we may not perish?" Then God saw their works, that they turned from their evil way: and God relented from the disaster that He had said He would bring upon them, and He did not do it."

A Word of Knowledge. This is the supernatural revelation by the Spirit of God of past or present facts. These facts are not something the possessor of the gift has already learned. They are totally unknown at the time they are revealed. They come directly from the infinite knowledge of God to the finite mind of the saint possessing this Gift. Where the Word of Wisdom always concerns future events, the Word of Knowledge always concerns past or present facts. It is the revelation of past or present events that can make change in present and future events.

The Word of Knowledge and the Word of Wisdom, though totally different, work together. They are at times used in the same message, being intertwined together, which sometimes makes them hard to distinguish. For example, look at Revelation 1-4. Jesus appears to John the beloved on the Isle of Patmos and tells him about the condition of the seven churches of Asia Minor. The conditions of these churches were revealed through the Word of Knowledge. Then the Lord went on to give John a Word of Wisdom for each church. God instructed John to inform the seven churches of Asia Minor of what they were doing and what they should do in the future to accomplish the plans and purposes He had set for them. Please notice Revelation 3:1-6 as one example.

> And to the angel of the church in Sardis write, 'these things saith He who has the seven Spirits of God and the seven stars: "I know your works, that you have a name that you are alive, but you are dead. Be watchful, and strengthen the things which remain, that are ready to die, for I have not found your works perfect before God. Remember therefore how you have received and heard; hold fast and repent. Therefore, if you will not watch, I will come upon you as a thief, and you will not know what hour I will come upon you. You have a few names even in Sardis who have not defiled their garments; and they shall walk with Me in white, for they are worthy. He who overcomes shall be clothed in white garments, and I will not

blot out his name from the Book of Life; but I will confess his name before My Father and before His angels. He who has an ear, let him hear what the Spirit says to the churches."

In this section of scripture, the Word of Wisdom and the Word of Knowledge are interwoven. Without careful study, it is hard to separate the two gifts used in this passage. Listed below are the Words of Knowledge

1. "I know your works, that you have a name that you are alive, but you are dead."
2. "Be watchful, and strengthen the things which remain, that are ready to die, for I have not found your works perfect before God."
3. "You have a few names even in Sardis who have not defiled their garments."

Now the Words of Wisdom contained in the same verses. Observe how the words of wisdom and knowledge are interwoven together, where one starts and the other ends.

1. "Therefore, if you will not watch, I will come upon you as a thief, and you will not know, what hour I will come upon you."
2. "He who overcomes shall be clothed in white garments, and I will not blot out his name from the Book of Life; but I will confess His name before My Father and before His angels."

Here are some biblical examples of the Word of Knowledge, which will help you understand how it is used, and for what purpose.

1. God gave a Word of Knowledge to Elisha concerning a hypocritical servant (2 Kings 5:20-27). Gehazi followed after Naaman because he lusted for payment after his master Elisha refused any for healing Naaman of Leprosy. Elisha received the Word of Knowledge from God on what Gehazi had done, and Gehazi received Naaman's Leprosy. God used the Word of Knowledge so that a man of God's reputation and ministry would not be brought into question, and to reveal sin in a ministry leader, so that the ministry would remain sanctified and holy before God.

2. God spoke to Elisha and revealed the King of Syria's plans to destroy Israel (2 Kings 6:9-12). In this story, the King of Syria kept making plans to make war against the people of God. Elisha was informed by God about the Syrian king's plans. Elisha then informed the King of Israel, who promptly thwarted the plans of the Syrian king.

3. God informed Samuel where Saul was hiding (1 Samuel 10:22). Samuel inquired of the Lord if the man should yet come forth, and the Lord gave Samuel a Word of Knowledge by telling him exactly where Saul was hiding. By revealing where Saul was, God once again confirmed to Samuel that Saul was to be king.

4. Jesus spoke to the women at the well of Sychar (John 4:18-29). This encounter saved the woman's soul. Jesus knew everything she ever did and he revealed some of it to her, which caused her to believe. This newfound faith in Christ caused an entire town to believe.

5. Peter spoke concerning the corruption in the early Church (Acts 5:1-17). Ananias and Sapphira his wife, tried to lie to the Holy Spirit. God revealed it to Peter and they both were rebuked and both died immediately. You cannot lie to the Spirit of God without retribution.

6. Ananias was informed by God regarding Saul's conversion and his blindness (Acts 9:10-17). God revealed to Ananias

exactly where Saul of Tarsus was being housed and that Ananias was to go there and pray for Saul. He was also informed that Saul had been converted. Saul was now confirmed before the body of Christ as a new creation in Christ and a man called of God.

7. Now I will share a modern-day example of the Word of Knowledge. While ministering in a small church in Mount Vernon, New York, the Lord informed me of the fact that some praise and worship ministers that had recently started coming to the church were there to separate the members of the congregation because they had just started their own church, and they needed members. The pastor was informed immediately and privately of this Word of Knowledge. Because of the church's need for a music ministry however, the Word was ignored. The explanation given was, "I'll pray about it and see what the Lord would say to do about it." As spiritual and proper as that sounds, it was wrong because the pastor used it as a patronizing gesture. During the month-long delay, congregation members were stolen, and partisanship developed among the remaining members. After a month of seeing what was taking place, the pastor asked the praise and worship leaders to leave, which they did, only after they had already taken a good number of members with them to their newly founded church.

One final word about the Word of Knowledge, the revelation that it brings is never about the future, but only about the past or present. The revelation of past or present events and/or facts is of tremendous benefit to the Church, because through it the Body of Christ can and will be purified. Distress will be comforted. Saints will be made joyful. Lost property will be found. The plans of the enemy will be revealed and laid waste. The people of God will be set free, and souls will be saved. Most important however, the Lord Jesus Christ will be glorified.

Discerning of spirits. This Gift completes the Group we call the Gifts of Revelation. Please notice what the Gift is called, Discerning of spirits. In contrast to the Word of Knowledge and the Word of Wisdom, which have an unlimited range of times and circumstance contained within its boundaries of operation, discerning of spirits possesses a much more limited range. Just like a great telescope that is synchronized in its movements to the revolution of a single planet or star, rather than to the entire universe, so is Discerning of spirits. Its powers of revelation are restricted to a single class of objects spirits, whether the spirits are from God, from the evil one, or our own spirit.

Discerning of spirits is not the gift of Discernment as many have taken it to mean. Discerning of spirits is the God given ability to distinguish spirits operating in any given situation. Discernment means to distinguish, or to separate out so as to investigate. It also means to examine, scrutinize, or to question. That in itself is fine, but it is incorrect to leave it at that point. Remember the Gift is called Discerning of spirits. The definition should correctly be, to distinguish, or to separate out so as to investigate, to examine, scrutinize, or to question the kind of spirit that is influencing actions taken by a person, persons, church, or ministry. This Gift includes recognizing spirits influencing entire cities, states, nations, or countries as well. As we are all aware, there are three kinds of spirits operating in the world today; the human spirit which is called the will, satanic, those spirits cast out of heaven because evil was found in them and divine Spirits, like Angels, and the Holy Spirit.

Here are some examples of the operation of the Gift of Discerning of spirits that might help clarify it further. We were ministering in Tyler, a small town in Texas. Tyler is ninety miles dead east of Dallas. Our ministry took us to the streets for street evangelism. For weeks, we were not making any noticeable progress, so the team decided to fast and pray for direction. During that time, the Lord informed us that we were combating religious controlling spirits, which had to be bound before we continued. The evangelistic team took the next few weeks, fasted and prayed that the religious spirits in control of the area, would be broken and the people set free from their influence. We once again hit the streets, only this time with remarkable results. People were receptive to the message. Others were healed, set free, and many saved.

Another remarkable incident happened in New York. One evening while we were ministering with a fellow evangelist in a church in Mount Vernon, the evangelist told us that she had seen a spirit of infirmity, which was called epilepsy, attached to a young man in the service. This young man was not known to her. The evangelist asked the young man to come up for prayer, and he responded. He informed us that for most of his life he would go into uncontrollable convulsions. He was seen by many doctors, trying many different medications with no success. The doctors classified him as an epileptic. We prayed for him as the Spirit of God instructed us to. We called out the spirit of epilepsy. The young man immediately fell to the floor in an epileptic seizure. We continued to pray calling out the evil spirit. After about ten minutes, the evil spirit let out a loud screech, and the convulsions immediately stopped. The young man remained perfectly still for a while, with a calm look on his face. When the young man got off the floor after about fifteen minutes, he was completely set free from the spirit of epilepsy.

We kept in touch with the young man for several years after that incident, and we are happy to report that he had not had another epileptic seizure since that meeting. He was no longer taking any prescribed medication, and he was now able to get a driver's license, which he was never allowed to have because of the epilepsy. In this case, the God given Gift of Discerning of spirits operating in conjunction with the omnipotence of God delivered this young man from an infirmity that had plagued him all his life. Give God all the praise for He is worthy!

To summarize, Discerning of spirits is not psychological insight, nor is it mind reading. It is not the power to discern faults, the ability to examine a person's character, or to expose the thoughts of the heart. It is not even the discerning of people, because all these actions are forbidden in scripture. "Judge not, that ye be not judged" (Matthew 7:1 KJV). The Gift is called Discerning of spirits, and it deals with spirits that operate in the realm of the spiritual. At the fear of being redundant let me point out that the Gift of Discerning of spirits is not just the discerning of evil spirits. It is supernatural insight into the spirit world. It deals with spirits that exist in the spirit realm, whether they are the human spirit, satanic, or divine. These different spirit forces influence us to manifest certain characteristics, whether they are good or evil, normal, or abnormal.

The uses of the Gift of Discerning of spirits are obvious, and the present-day uses are the same as they were throughout biblical history.

1. Discerning of spirits helps in delivering the afflicted, oppressed, and tormented. Demon possession and oppression is responsible today for more cases of mental disorders than most people realize. Minds are still wrecked and driven by "cruel, tormenting spirits" (Mark 5:5; Luke 9:39), where people are still driven into rages, forced into acts of violence that seem incomprehensible, or encouraged to commit the greatest of offenses of self-destruction. Youthful hearts are driven by "unclean spirits" (Acts 5:16) to revolting talk and obscene behavior which result in incurable diseases. The power of speech is robbed by "dumb spirits," the light of day is darkened by "blind spirits," and the voices of beloved friends are muted by "deaf spirits" (Matthew 12:22; Mark 9:17, 25). Entire bodies or individual limbs are distorted and twisted by "spirits of infirmity" (Luke 13:11, 16). These are not only illnesses that doctors or psychotherapists are equipped to handle. Any believer who possesses the Gift of Discerning of spirits and who

is operating in the power of God is not only equipped to handle those under Satan's power but are commanded to do so and by obeying God, cure them.

Some of you may be asking right now, "Is this preacher saying that all sickness and disease are due to evil spirits?" No, not at all! The Scriptures make it quite clear that many are. The Gift of Discerning of spirits working in conjunction with the other Gifts of the Spirit are for distinguishing which are and which are not. It is only through the Gift of Discerning of spirits that we are able to tell whether an infirmity is a result of a non-functioning component, demon oppression, or God's judgment. For example, a deaf ear can be caused by a shattered eardrum, severe damage to the acoustic nerve, or one can have a healthy well-functioning acoustic system that is held captive in the grasp of an evil oppressing spirit, or it could be as the result of God's judgment (Numbers 12).

All sickness whether of mind or body is represented in the Scriptures as oppression. Oppression simply means to exercise control over, whether that control is taken by God which we call God's judgment (Numbers 12; Acts 12:21-25), or control taken by the devil (Acts 10:38; Luke 13:16). This control can be over the actions, which cause an illness or over the illness itself. For example, everyone knows how addictive smoking can be, that is oppression. Lung cancer, the natural result of smoking, is not necessarily the work of an oppressing demon, but due in fact to the unhealthy practice of smoking.

Diabetes is another such example. In our ministry as well as other well renowned Spirit filled ministries, there are many documented accounts of individuals with diabetes who are set free from a spirit of diabetes. On the other hand, we have obesity, which is due to the uncontrolled and undisciplined consumption of food (which is evil oppression) that causes diabetes. Once food consumption is controlled and proper medical procedures followed, diabetes often subsides. Brethren, whether oppression is the cause or the effect, we must understand that the authority of the. Holy Spirit has dominion over all areas of a person's being whether it be spiritual, physical, or psychological. Discerning of spirits allows us to know over which area the demon is controlling. As a result of that knowledge, we know exactly how to enact a cure.

2. Discerning of spirits helps in discovering a servant of the devil (Acts 13:8-12). Imagine being at work or at church and there is a person who, when they come near, you feel oppressed. When the person comes around, immediately your joy leaves. This person is also the one that causes you the most trouble and is always in your face when you make an error. This person could be your boss, a coworker, or even a family member. Wouldn't it be a blessing to understand exactly what is prompting this person to act in such a way? Wouldn't it be easier to pray and set that person free if you knew what evil spirit was at work in him? Wouldn't it be a blessing to recognize an evil spirit at work in your church? Or it could be there are evil spirits that are at work restricting the praise and worship, or even the operation of the Gifts themselves? What about the blessing of being able to recognize false Christ's, false prophets, false teachers, false apostles, or false brethren! When the Gift of Discerning of spirits is in operation, the ability to recognize these false deceiving spirits will enable us not to be turned aside by every wind of doctrine. Through the Gift of Discerning of spirits, servants of the devil are recognizable.

3. Discerning of spirits aids in checking the plans of the adversary. In Acts 16:16-18, it is interesting to note that the Greek term for the "spirit of divination" (Acts 16:16), is puthon—which was an oracle represented by a python.

Divination is soothsaying or witchcraft. These demons inspire idolatry. Look at whom Revelation 12:9 calls the serpent. "So, the great dragon was cast out, that serpent of old, called the devil and Satan, who deceives the whole world; he was cast to the earth, and his angels were cast out with him." The devil kills and destroys; we all know that. How then will Satan's attempts at destroying us be avoided? We avoid them by the Gift of Discerning of spirits. Through this Gift, we can recognize the attacker and stop his attacks in their earliest stages.

4. Discerning of spirits aid in unmasking demon miracle workers (2 Thessalonians 2:9). Wherever there is God's power and truth there must be satanic "signs and lying wonders. "The most substantial proof of the existence of the divine, are the satanic signs and lying wonders. The success of the counterfeit is in its likeness to the real. Apart from the Gifts of Discerning of spirits the very elect themselves would be deceived by "spirits of devils, working miracles" (See Revelation 16:14).

One example of satanic signs and lying wonders can be found in Exodus 7 and 8. The first three miracles that God performed through Moses, Moses' rod turning into a serpent, the water turning into blood, and the plaque of frogs were all duplicated by Pharaoh's magicians. It was not until the fourth plague, the plague of lice, that the magicians realized and informed pharaoh that these signs were the work of the one true living God. The revelation came when the magicians could not duplicate or stop it by their incantations and magical powers. "Now the magicians so worked with their enchantments to bring forth lice, but they could not. So, there were lice on man and beast. Then the magicians said to Pharaoh, `This is the finger of God.' However, Pharaoh's heart grew hard, and he did not heed them, just as the LORD had said" (Exodus 8:18-19).

5. Discerning of spirits also aids us in exposing errors in doctrine (1st Timothy 4:1, 2 Peter 2:1). "Seducing spirits," and "lying spirits," are responsible for the "doctrines of devils" and "damnable heresies." There are many of these "lying spirits and "doctrines of devils" coming through men and women dressed up in robes, and standing in pulpits all over the world. We were told this would happen. 2 Timothy 4:3-4 says, "For the time will come when they will not endure sound doctrine, but according to their own desires, because they have itching ears, they will heap up for themselves teachers; who will turn their ears away from the truth, and be turned aside to fables." Many will turn their ears away from the truth, and be turned aside to fables. Why? Because they are content being lazy. They would rather let someone in a robe, standing in a pulpit tell them what truth is. Rather than, take the time, and effort to properly study God's Word. Why do you think the command is given to "be diligent to present yourself approved to God, a worker who does not need to be ashamed, rightly dividing the word of truth" (2 Timothy 2:15)?

There was a man I knew that loved to debate the Bible; he once told me that he had never studied it and wasn't sure what I was telling him about it was the truth. I gave him Scripture references to look up, which would prove that I was telling him the truth. He objected by saying, he would not look them up because he would then become responsible for the knowledge. When I asked him to explain what he meant, he told me that in his religion the priest is responsible for telling him the truth. It is his responsibility to obey the priest, that's all. If the priest is wrong then the priest would be held responsible for leading him astray. If he looked them up however, he, first, would be disobedient to the priest and second, he would be responsible for what he discovered. He would therefore let the priest tell him what truth is, that way God could not hold him responsible for any wrongdoing. Sounds silly doesn't it! A good number of Christians today, maybe without realizing it, do the exact same thing. When was the last time you spent a good amount of time studying, not just reading, but studying the Bible? When was the last time you looked up in the Bible the truthfulness of the information your priest or pastor was delivering?

A pastor friend of ours who had a large church in Beaumont, Texas told us that the Lord had ordered him and his elders to go on a twenty-one day fast. On the last day of the fast, he was instructed to hold an all-day church prayer meeting. At that prayer meeting, the pastor and the elders of the church were given a similar vision, which he related to us. The vision was of a man running through a lake of fire, reaching down into the flames and pulling up people by their hair. The man would then look at the face and throw them back down into the flames. The pastor and the elders, filled with horror and shock, began to earnestly seek the face of the Lord for the interpretation of the vision. The Lord responded by telling them that the man running through the flames was a parishioner of a church, searching for his pastor who had steered him wrong.

The moral of these stories is that we cannot depend on anyone, except Christ through the Holy Spirit to lead us to all truth. This is not to say that we are not to seek out true God-fearing pastors and leaders, for God commands us to gather ourselves together (Hebrews 10: 25) under God ordained leaders. Remember apostles, prophets, evangelists, pastors, and teachers are gifts sent by God to care for the body of Christ (refer, Ephesians 4:12-16). If we become lazy or allow unbelief, complacency, and fear to restrict us from searching out the revelation of truth, either by prayerful study or through God ordained leaders, it opens the door for "lying spirits" and "doctrines of devils." Be reminded that the devil may appear as an angel of light (2 Corinthians 11:14). If we do not pray for the Gift of "Discerning of spirits," which allows us to recognize him and his "modus operandi" (his mode of operation), we warrant the same fate as the man running through the flames searching for the pastor that steered him wrong.

At this point, I would suggest you read 2 Timothy 2:15 and 2 Timothy 4:3-4 again and discover what these Scriptures say. Are you depending on someone else to tell you what he or she thinks truth is, or are you studying to show yourself approved to God, letting God tell you exactly what truth is? We are not saying that you should never attend church or listen to the pastor, God Forbid! (Read Romans 10:14 and Hebrews 10:25.) What we are saying is that we should never take for granted that everything coming out of the pulpit, whether it is in our church, on television, or on radio, be taken at face value. What is being preached should be examined, and studied for its validity as truth. Jesus said that the Holy Spirit will lead you to all truth (John 10:13-14). Pray over every message you hear and let the Holy Spirit confirm what is being proclaimed as truth.

If more Christians would earnestly seek God for the operation of the Gift of Discerning of spirits, imagine how many souls would be saved from error, in the wake of people like Theudas in Acts 5:36, Jim Jones (Jonestown), David Koresh (Waco, Texas), Sun Myung Moon (the Unitarian Church), Joseph Smith Jr. (Mormonism), Charles Tate Russell (Jehovah Witnesses), Mary Baker Eddy (Christian Science), Herbert W. Armstrong (the World Tomorrow), and countless others.

Dearly beloved, the very existence of the Gift of Discerning of spirits proves beyond a shadow of a doubt, the very present reality of evil spirits. They are wrecking and torturing human lives as cruelly as in the Lord's Day. Look at the newspaper or watch television, and way too often you will see the evil that men do. The inhuman cruelties that are inflicted on others by evil men, women, and children are all influenced and driven by evil spirits. Until Jesus returns, we are in a deadly, non-ending war for the eternal souls of man. This war waged by lying and seducing spirits has already destroyed and is now destroying countless millions. If we do not have our eyes opened like Elisha's servant at Dothan (2 Kings 6:13-17), we will all suffer tremendous and devastating losses.

We must, in the face of all the evil around us, seek earnestly such Gifts as will liberate those enslaved and tormented by the devil's power. They are the ones for whom Christ died! It is unbelief, complacency, fear, and the overwhelming desire for peace that is now holding Christendom in a state of false ease and comfort, while at the same time, not allowing its armies to go out and rescue those being held behind the gates of hell. For do you not know, brethren that the gates of hell shall not prevail against "us" (Matthew 16:28b). "And that God has given us the keys of the kingdom of heaven, and whatever we bind on earth will be bound in heaven, and whatever we lose on earth will be loosed in heaven" (Matthew 16:29). He did not give us this authority to stand idly by and do nothing. Let us, therefore,

> Put on the whole armor of God that you may be able to stand against the wiles of the devil. For we do not wrestle against flesh and blood, but against principalities, against powers, against the rulers of the darkness of this age, against spiritual hosts of wickedness in the heavenly places. Therefore, take up the whole armor of God that you may be able to withstand in the evil day, and having done all, to stand"
>
> Ephesians 6:11-13

In this particular group of Gifts, God through the Spirit reveals information that is beneficial for instruction and guidance. This information spans a wide variety of areas, such as spiritual, physical, emotional, and psychological. The information that is revealed to the finite knowledge of man comes straight from the infinite wisdom and foreknowledge of God and can pertain to the past, present, or future. This information can be general (regarding a group, church, city, state, nation, etc.) or specific (regarding an individual). Lord, let your love so drive us to desperately desire these Gifts. Not for our own benefit but for all those afflicted by evil. Amen!

This completes our study on the Gifts of Revelation. God reveals, through the Word of Knowledge certain information regarding the past and present, through the Word of Wisdom information is given concerning the future, and by Discerning of spirits we have the ability to detect and recognize spirits, which allows us to operate safely in the spiritual realm.

Chapter Questions To
Help Your Study

1. What is the most important thing to remember about the Spiritual Gifts?
2. The Word of Wisdom always concerns future events that surround a person or people, a place or places, or a thing or things. True or False
3. The Word of Wisdom is for the unfolding of His unrevealed will and the declaration of His hidden purposes apart from His Word. True or False
4. The Word of Wisdom will however give us a small glimpse into the future. It is not a gift of utterance but of _____.
5. Give some biblical examples of the Word of Wisdom.
6. The Word of Wisdom once pronounced is not written in stone, the outcome can be changed. True or False
7. The Word of Knowledge always concerns past or present facts. True or False
8. The Word of Knowledge and the Word of Wisdom, though totally different, can work together. True or False
9. Give some biblical examples of the Word of Knowledge.
10. "Discerning of spirits" possesses a much more limited range than the other two. True or False
11. "Discerning of spirits" is not a psychological insight, nor is it mind reading. It is not the power to discern faults, character, or the thoughts of the heart; it is not even the discerning of people. True or False
12. Give some uses for the Gift of Discernment.

THE GIFTS OF POWER

We have now come to the second group of Spiritual Gifts, "The Gifts of Power." Among these are Healing, Miracles, and Faith. These are referred to as the Power Gifts because they create, generate, or produce something. They are supernatural in origin, and they go far beyond any and all abilities of man.

1. The Gifts of Healings (Acts 3:1-9).
   Now Peter and John went up together to the temple at the hour of prayer, the ninth hour. And a certain man lame from his mother's womb was carried, whom they laid daily at the gate of the temple which is called Beautiful, to ask alms from those who entered the temple; who, seeing Peter and John about to go into the temple, asked for alms. And fixing his eyes on him, with John, Peter said, "Look at us." So, he gave them his attention, expecting to receive something from them. Then Peter said, "Silver and gold I do not have, but what I do have I give you: In the name of Jesus Christ of Nazareth, rise up and walk." And he took him by the right hand and lifted him up, and immediately his feet and ankle bones received strength. So, he leaping up, stood and walked and entered the temple with them—walking, leaping, and praising God. And all the people saw him walking and praising God.

No ability of man could have ever immediately given the man's feet and ankle bones enough strength, so that for the first time in his entire life he could, without any previous practice walk, and leap into the air.

2. The Gift of Miracles (Joshua 10:12-14).
The LORD delivered up the Amorites before the children of Israel, and he said in the sight of Israel, "Sun, stand still over Gibeon; And Moon, in the Valley of Aijalon." So, the sun stood still. And the moon stopped till the people had revenge upon their enemies. Is this not written in the Book of Jasher? So, the sun stood still in the midst of heaven, and did not hasten to go down for about a whole day. And there has been no day like that, before it or after it that the LORD heeded the voice of a man; for the LORD fought for Israel.

Even in this age of unlimited technological advancements, we do not possess the ability to make the sun stand still or make the moon stop in its orbit. This was truly a miracle brought about by the power of an omnipotent God, who heard the prayer of His faithful servant Joshua.

3. The Gift of Faith (Daniel 3:13-18).
Then Nebuchadnezzar, in rage and fury, gave the command to bring Shadrach, Meshach, and Abed-Nego. So, they brought these men before the king. Nebuchadnezzar spoke, saying to them, "Is it true, Shadrach, Meshach, and Abed-Nego that you do not serve my gods or worship the gold image which I have set up?" Now if you are ready at the time you hear the sound of the horn, flute, harp, lyre, and psaltery, in symphony with of music, and you

fall down and worship the image which I have made, good! But if you do not worship, you shall be cast immediately into the midst of a burning fiery furnace. And who is the god who will deliver you from my hands?" Shadrach, Meshach and Abed-Nego answered and said to the king, "O Nebuchadnezzar, we have no need to answer you in this matter." If that is the case, our God whom we serve is able to deliver us from the burning fiery, furnace and He will deliver us from your hand, O king. But if not, let it be known to you O king that we do not serve your gods, nor will we worship the gold image which you have set up.

Shadrach, Meshach, and Abed-Nego had supernatural faith to believe that their God would save them from the burning fiery furnace one way or another. They came out of the fiery furnace with no injuries whatsoever. They didn't even smell like smoke, which is something that many Christians today, cannot say.

Now that an example of each has been given, let's examine the Power Gifts more thoroughly.

The Gifts of Healings.

First, we must notice the important plurality in its title. It is not the Gift of Healing; it is the Gifts of Healings. In 1 Corinthians 12 the original language, puts the two nouns "Gifts and Healings" in the plural form (verses 9, 28, 30) Therefore, they will be referred to as such throughout this study. The reason for these two nouns being plural, is not found anywhere in the Scriptures. Many notable colleagues with a healing ministry believe that there are different gifts for different types of diseases. They have noted that they have relatively good success healing certain types of diseases while little or no success in healing others. One such example can be found in the ministry of Smith Wigglesworth. We know that this man of God was used to raise at least three people from the dead. It was said of him by his close friend and ministry partner, Charles Duncombe, that any time he found someone, who was inflicted with a goiter, Mr. Wigglesworth got all excited because he had great success with that type of affliction because he never saw a goiter he could not heal.[13]

Another such example is Kenneth E. Hagin who wrote in his book on the Holy Spirit and the Gifts that:

> ...in my own ministry, ruptures, growths, hernias, or lumps of any kind are almost always healed when I pray for people. I once kept a record in every meeting I had over a period of several years. And in ninety-nine cases out of one hundred, these types of afflictions were eventually all healed.[14]

Although there is no explanation in scripture for the words "gifts," and "healings" being plural, one thing is known about the Gifts, that is, that they are for the supernatural healing of diseases without natural means. They are miraculous manifestations of the Spirit of God for the elimination of all human ills whether they are organic, functional, nervous, acute, or chronic in nature, and these Gifts of Healings are freely given to all believers.

The Lord Himself brought the Gifts of Healings into prominence with His innumerable acts of Healings and other works (John 21:25). He made "healing the sick" part of the great commission (Mark 16:15-18). He also told His disciples that "healing the sick" should go along with the preaching of the Gospel (Matthew 10:7-8) and that the preaching of the Gospel would be confirmed by the Gifts of Healings as well as other signs (Mark 16:18-20).

Here are some other purposes for the Gifts of Healings.

1. To destroy the works of the devil in the human body (Matthew 8:3-7; Acts 10:38).
2. To establish Jesus' claims of who He is (John 10:36-38).
3. To establish the resurrection (Acts 3:15-16).
4. To draw people closer to Jesus (John 6:2).
5. To bring glory to God (Mark 2:12, Luke 13:17).

The Gifts of Healings can be seen operating in several different ways.

1. By the faith of the minister (Matthew 8:16, 9:25; Mark 5:21-43; Luke 4:18). This can include anointing with oil and the laying on of hands.
2. By the faith of the individual (Matthew 9:27-29; Mark 5:24-34; Luke 18:35-43). This can include individual actions such as stretching forth a withered arm (Matthew 12:10-13), taking up your bed and walking (John 5:1-9), washing in a river (2 Kings 5:1-10), or a pool (John 9:1-11).
3. Intercession; the Prayer of Faith (Matthew 8:5-13, 9:18-22; 15:22-28; Mark 2:1-5, 9:20-22; James 5:15-16).
4. Use of inanimate objects like Peter's shadow (Acts 5:13-15), or Paul's handkerchief (Acts 19:11-12).

The Gifts of Healings are ministered by men who are anointed by the Holy Spirit. One essential element in ministering the Gifts of Healings is faith. Faith is the indispensable essential fuel in healing, and it is important to point out that the Gifts do not work indiscriminately at the will of the possessor. Not every blind, deaf, or sick man can be healed at will. Bethesda's porches were filled with the sick, and they were all believers in divine healing, for they were all waiting for an angel to stir up the waters so that they could receive their miracle of healing (John 5). The minister on that occasion was the Lord Himself, the one supremely gifted with the power of the Spirit to heal. Yet only one was actually healed, the one who actually came into contact with the Master Himself. In other words, all healings are by the Spirit as the Spirit wills and when He wills (1 Corinthians 7:1-12). This is also confirmed in 1 Corinthians 12, where six times in the first twelve verses, the Holy Spirit is said to be the one who gives and operates the Gifts as He wills, when He wills, and by the one that He wills.

One last point, not everyone is given, the Gifts of Healings. They, again, are as the Spirit wills. Notice 1 Corinthians 12:27-30.

"Now you are the body of Christ, and members individually. And God has appointed these in the church: first apostles, second prophets, third teachers, after that miracles, then gifts of healings, helps, administrations, varieties of tongues. Are all apostles? Are all prophets? Are all teachers? Are all workers of miracles? Do all have gifts of healings? Do all speak with tongues? Do all interpret?"

Obviously, the answer Paul was alluding to was no. They were not all apostles or prophets or teachers. Therefore, it logically follows that; they all do not work miracles or have the Gifts of Healings. We are only vessels that the Holy Spirit uses, if we are available to be used. It is a well-known fact that God is not looking for ability but for availability! If you wish to be used of God in any area including this one, it stands to reason, that first you must believe, second you must be available, and third you must be given the Gift itself.

How does someone know if he possesses the Gifts of Healings? You may think that the answer to this commonly asked question is extremely complicated and filled with a good number of tests and steps to follow. Some ministers go as far as to sell books explaining the answer to this question. They even give you a step-by-step format to follow. Nevertheless, the truthful answer is not complicated; it doesn't take an entire book filled with tests and steps to follow to know if you have this Gift. On the contrary, it is quite simple.

"Go ye into all the world, and preach the gospel to every creature. He that believeth and is baptized shall be saved; but he that believeth not shall be damned. *And these signs shall follow them that believe;* In my name shall they cast out devils; they shall speak with new tongues; They shall take up serpents; and if they drink any deadly thing, it shall not hurt them; *they shall lay hands on the sick, and they shall recover.*" Mark 16:15-18, KJV

Notice the two italicized sections of this passage. Taken together they tell us that these signs follow obedience, one of those signs is healing. Are you in prayerful obedience to this commission? If so, do you see God using you to heal those you pray for? Do you live your life in a perpetual state of availability to God and find God making you acutely aware of strangers with infirmities? Do you find the boldness to pray for them and they get healed? Then it is a good possibility that you have the Gifts of Healings. On the other hand, if you are not in prayerful obedience to this commission, how can you possibly know if you have it or not? Apostle Ron Miller of the Salt Covenant Network once said to me, "If a person wants to see the miraculous, he must go. If he does not go, the miraculous is a no go!"

The Working of Miracles.

Before we can clearly approach any study on the Working of Miracles and before we can even attempt a precise definition, we must take a careful and comprehensive look at the word "miracle" itself. Professor T. H. Huxley expressed the need of a precise definition when he wrote:

> The first step in this, as in all other discussions, is to come to a clear understanding as to the meaning

> of the term employed. Argumentation whether miracles are possible, and if possible, credible, is mere beating the air until the arguers have agreed what they mean by the word "miracle."[15]

The general idea is that a miracle is something wonderful or unusual an event, experience, or discovery as singular and strange as to awaken in one the feeling of awe. For example, a phenomenon of nature and even events in history are often labeled "miracles." If a friend escapes death in a plane or car crash, we are apt to say, "it was a miracle that he was not killed." Often the ordinary course of nature is referred to as a miracle of God. Using the word miracle to define events like these has cheapened the depth of the meaning of the word.

What exactly is the definition of the word miracle? A miracle is a work wrought by a divine power, for a divine purpose, by means that are beyond the comprehension and ability of man. Miracles are works that are contrary to the laws of nature. Webster's definition of a miracle is clear and concise: "an event or effect in the physical laws of nature, or transcending our knowledge of these laws, an extraordinary, anomalous, or abnormal event brought about by a super-human agency"(Emphasis added).[16] Herbert Lockyer defined a miracle by saying, "The biblical conception of a miracle is that of some extraordinary work of deity transcending the ordinary powers of nature and wrought in connection with the ends of revelation"[17] (Emphasis added). Harold Horton also gives a definition of a miracle.

> A miracle is a sovereign act of the Spirit of God irrespective of laws or systems. A miracle does not, as some cynical unbelievers say, demand the existence of an undiscovered law to explain it. A miracle has no explanation other than the sovereign power of the Lord. God is not bound by His own

laws. God acts as He wills either within or outside of what we understand to be laws [e.g. Gravity], whether natural or supernatural. When in a sudden and sovereign act God steps outside the circle by which His creatures or creation are bordered, we call it a miracle. So, does God in the Scriptures.[18]

Now let's take our definition of miracle one step further. In any phase of Bible study, a close examination of the words used in the original language is vastly important for a fuller understanding of the meaning of any text or word. For this reason, we will now consider three words that are used to refer to miracles in their original languages in an attempt to better illuminate with true clarity and depth the definition of a Miracle and thereby help to further define the Gift of "Working of Miracles.

Teras. "Wonders"

This word indicates the state of mind produced on the eyewitnesses by the sight of miracles. Not the miracles themselves, but the state of mind produced by the miracle. In other words, to marvel, experience astonishment, or be in awe. The extraordinary character of a miracle demonstrates to all who witness it the reality and closeness of God to His people. To behold, such a display of power is contrary to previous expectation and opposite to any natural law with which people are familiar. Such miracles, however, are not to be regarded merely as "wonders," producing a momentary amazement but so that attention would be given to the author of the miracle, to their purpose, and to their inner spiritual appeal. Frederic Louis Godet a twentieth century biblical theologian expressed his opinion on their purpose by saying;

> The miracles of Jesus are not mere prodigies (Greek-teras) intended to strike the imagination. There

is a close relation between these marvelous facts and the person of Him who does them. They are visible emblems of what He is and what He comes to do, images which spring as rays from the abiding miracle of the manifestation of Christ.[19]

One word of warning must be given at this point. Although the word "teras" or wonders" is used thirteen times in the New Testament, only nine times does it refer to the divine manifestation and operation of God. Four times it refers to the manifestation and operation of the devil through human agents (Matthew 24:24, Mark 13:22, and 2 Thessalonians 2:9-10). These manifestations and operations are called lying signs and wonders. Many will follow these counterfeit miracles because as 2 Thessalonians 2:10b explains, "they received not the love of the truth, that they might be saved." (See Exodus 7:11, 22; 8:7; 2 John 7; Revelation 13:11-16; 16:12-14; 19:20.) How can you know what is and is not of God? The simple answer is: Know God—Know truth, No God—No truth. The Bible tells us that the Spirit of God will lead us to all truth (John 16:13). The Holy Spirit comes only when He is invited to come. Call on God, therefore, repent of your sins (Acts 17:13), invite Christ into your life and live righteously (Revelation 3:20), and the Holy Spirit of God will bear witness to the truth (Romans 8:6). Then pray and study God's word to find truth. Jesus said; "Sanctify them through thy truth: thy word is truth" (John 17:17). (Ref. 2 Timothy 3:16-17.)

Semeion. "Signs"

Here we have a word carrying with it a particular reference to the significance of miracles, again, not the miracle itself but the significance produced as a result of the miracle. The difference between a sign and a wonder is that a sign is intended to appeal to the understanding, whereas a wonder appeals to the imagination. Signs are seals, or credentials, by which God authenticates Himself as the miracle worker. A sign was to be looked upon as a token or indication of the near presence and working of God and as proof of His genuineness and His revelation. For example, the rainbow that was placed in the sky by God was given to Noah as an eternal sign or stamp of an everlasting covenant in which God promised never to destroy the earth again by a flood (Genesis 9:12-14). Every time we see a rainbow, we understand that God is reaffirming His everlasting covenant. Circumcision is another such sign (Genesis 17:10-11).

The miracles of Christ were signs, marks or pledges indicating someone greater than the signs themselves existed. Isaiah 7:11 says, "Ask a sign for yourself from the LORD your God; ask it either in the depth or in the height above." Isaiah 38:7 says, "And this is the sign to you from the LORD, that the LORD will do this thing which He has spoken." Signs are legitimate acts, whereby the miracle worker could claim to be God's representative.

> When the men had come to Him, they said, "John the Baptist has sent us to You, saying, Are You the Coming One, or do we look for another?" And that very hour He cured many of infirmities, afflictions, and evil spirits; and to many who were blind He gave sight. Jesus answered and said to them, "Go and tell John the things you have seen and heard: that the blind see, the lame walk, the lepers are cleansed, the deaf hear, the dead are raised, the poor have the gospel preached to them.
>
> Luke 7:20-22

Romans 15:19 says, "Through mighty signs and wonders, by the power of the Spirit of God; so that from Jerusalem, and round about unto Illyricum, I have fully preached the gospel of Christ."

1 Corinthians 2:4-5 states, "And my speech and my preaching was not with enticing words of man's wisdom, but in demonstration

of the Spirit and of power: That your faith should not stand in the wisdom of men, but in the power of God."

Dunamis. "Powers"

Dunamis is translated "miracles" as well as "powers" throughout the New Testament. It is the power or the intrinsic ability of supernatural origin and character used to do works above and totally separate from the natural abilities of man. Miracles manifest the mighty power of God, which was inherent in Christ Himself, "the great power of God" (Acts 8:10). Simply stated the word "teras" or "Wonders" refers to the state of mind produced in the eyewitnesses by the sight of miracles, or the astonishment or awe the eyewitness feels. Semeion refers to the significance produced as a result of the miracle. Signs give authority or credentials to the one bringing forth the miracles, where dunamis points to the supernatural source of the miracle, God Himself. Dunamis is translated "wonderful works" in Matthew 7:22, "mighty works" in Matthew 11:20; Mark 6:14; and Luke 10:13, or "miracles" in Acts 2:22, 19:11; 1 Corinthians 12:10, 28: and Galatians 3:5.

All three of these words examined above are used in one verse: Acts 2:22. Let us look at this verse so we can get a clear understanding of what exactly the purpose of miracles is.

> Men of Israel, hear these words: Jesus of Nazareth, a Man attested by God to you by miracles [dunamesin], wonders [terasin], and signs [semeiois], which God did through Him in your midst, as you yourselves also know.

Notice carefully to what these three words point as the only purpose of miracles. That purpose is to attest, to certify and to verify, to the entire world, that Jesus Christ of Nazareth is the only means, God has given to mankind for the salvation of their souls. Read the rest of Acts 2 and also 1 Timothy 2:5-6 for more clarification; "For there is one God and one mediator between God and men, the man Christ Jesus, who gave Himself a ransom for all, to be testified in due time."

Before closing our discussion on the gift of "Working of Miracles, we must consider first, what are the divisions of miracles? And second, what are the uses of miracles?

1. What are the divisions of miracles?
   A. Power of Nature.
      - Parting of the Red Sea (Exodus 14).
      - Floating of an iron axe head (2 Kings 6:5-6).
      - Calling fire from heaven at Mt. Camel (1 Kings 18).
      - Stopping the Sun in the sky, for a day (Joshua 10:12-13).
      - Walking on Water (Matthew 14).
      - Stilling of the Storm (Matthew 8:26-27).

   B. Power over Disease.
      - Healing leprosy (Matthew 8:3).
      - Healed the Paralytic Man (Matthew 9:2~).
      - Opened blind eyes (Luke 7:20-22.)
      - Opened closed ears (Mark 9:25).
      - Healing the dumb (Matthew 15:31, Mark 9:25).
      - Healing a withered hand (Luke 6:610).

   C. Power over Death.
      - Enoch missed death (Genesis 5:21-24).
      - Elijah missed death (2 Kings 2:11).
      - Killed Nadab and Abihu (Leviticus 10:1-2).
      - Lazarus rose from the dead (John 11:38 44).
      - Death of Ananias and Sapphira (Acts 5:1-10).
      - Jesus rose from the dead (Matthew 28:1-7).

D. Power over Demons.
- Boy with the Mute Spirit (Mark 9:17~)
- Mary Magdalene (Luke 8:2~).
- Man, in tombs at Gergesenes (Matthew 8:28~).
- Blind and Mute man (Matthew 12:22~)
- Lunatic Boy (Luke 9:38~)
- Man possessed in the synagogue (Luke 4:31~).

2. What are the uses of miracles?
  A. For Divine Deliverance.
  - Escape from Egypt (Exodus 3~)

  B. Provision for those in need.
  - Feeding of the Multitude (Matthew 14:13)

  C. To carry out divine judgment.
  - Nadab and Abihu (Leviticus 10:12)
  - Ananias and Sapphira (Acts 5:1-I0)

  D. To confirm the preached Word of God.
  - Elymas the sorcerer (Acts 13:8-12)
  - Mark 16:20.

  E. For deliverance from the unavoidable situations of danger.
  - Sudden tempest on the Sea (Matthew 8:23)

  F. To raise the dead.
  - Lazarus (John 11:38-44)
  - The widow of Nain's son (Luke 7:11-14)

  G. To display God's power and magnificence.
  - Jesus' (Matthew 11:1-5; John 5:36-38, 10:25)

- Elijah the Prophet (2 Kings 1:9~)
- Elijah the Prophet (2 Kings 18:18)

The Gift of Faith

The "Gift of Faith," is doubtless the greatest and most confusing of the three Gifts of Power. One reason is that the "Gift of Faith" is only one of the four faiths found in Scripture. Another reason is that the Greek word used for all four "Faiths" is the same, "Pistis." This makes the study of these types of faith very difficult. Many believers misunderstand which faith is being used in a certain passage, and confuse where one faith ends and the other begins. For example, even though a person might have faith to believe the Bible, it does not necessarily mean he has saving faith. And even though a person has saving faith, which can only come as a gift from God, it doesn't necessarily mean he has the "Gift of Faith" described in 1 Corinthians 12. So, with that in mind, it is essential that we identify and clarify the differences between these four Faiths.

The four faiths are:

1. Natural or General Faith
2. Saving Faith
3. The "Fruit of Faith" or Faithfulness
4. The "Gift of Faith"

1. Natural or General Faith.

Natural Faith is God given (Romans 12:3), in the same way as natural wisdom. This Natural or General Faith is quite distinct from every form of divine faith whether miraculous or non-miraculous. Natural Faith is that which, the farmer exercises when he sows seed, and the husbandman uses when he waits for the precious fruit of the earth. And is the same faith we exercise every evening when we lie down to sleep after making plans for the next day. We fall asleep fully believing we will see the next day, even though God tells us, "Come now, you who say, Today or tomorrow we will go to such and such a city, spend a year there, buy and sell, and make a profit'; whereas you do not know what will happen tomorrow. For what is your life? It is even a vapor that appears for a little time and then vanishes away" (James 4:12-14).

Natural or General Faith is the type of faith that every person has inside them. It does not save, even when it receives the facts of Jesus' life and death. It is the faith found in the head via repetition and acquaintance: whereas saving faith is of the heart. Believing the record that God gave His Son (1 John 5:10) means not only nodding mental assent, but to step beyond natural faith into the realm of commitment; or what is called "Saving Faith." Saving Faith demands 24/7 commitment to Christ and His Word.

Let me illustrate this point. A number of years ago a man placed a tight rope over Niagara Falls. This act drew much media attention. The first day the man proceeded to walk across the falls on the tight rope using a long wooden rod for balance. The second day, to the crowd's wonderment, he walked across the falls without the long wooden rod. The third day with the crowd in amazement he proceeded to walk across Niagara Falls pushing a wheel barrel. Each day before demonstrating his wondrous talent, he asked the crowd if they believed he could do it. The crowd responded with a resounding, yes! The fourth day the man placed two hundred pounds of sand in the wheel barrel. He asked the crowd again if they believed he could make it across the falls. The crowd once again, responded with a resounding, yes, we believe! The last day of this marvelous exhibition, the man asked the crowd if they believed he could put a person in the wheel barrel and make it across the falls. The crowd enthusiastically cried out, yes! Nevertheless, when he asked the multitude of onlookers that had gathered over the previous few days for a volunteer, not one person volunteered to step into the wheel barrel.

This is a perfect example of the difference between Natural or General Faith and Saving Faith. We believe in our minds but are unwilling to put our lives on the line for what we believe and act according to what we say we believe.

Natural or General Faith is the type of faith that most people who attend church today have in Christ. They believe He is who He says He is. They believe He died for them. They even believe in heaven, and for the most part, they believe in hell. But this type of faith does not bring salvation. Remember demons have this kind of faith to perfection. "They believe and tremble" (James 2:19). They have a conviction amounting to positive certainty, concerning the things that most people who attend church believe, that is why they tremble. Demons, however, just like many people who attend church, are not saved. Having Saving Faith would be paramount to stepping into the wheel barrel.

2. "Saving Faith."

Saving faith is when you voluntarily place your life in God's hands, letting Christ live through you. In other words, one must give credibility and authority to the moral conviction of religious truths, or the truthfulness of God. Above all, it means total reliance upon Christ for salvation and being consistent in that profession. God calls that consistency "faithfulness."

Although it is true that Saving Faith is a gift of God and the same Greek word is used in 1 Corinthians 12 for the Gift of Faith, it is distinct from Saving Faith. Saving faith is a divine gift needed before and imperative for salvation. On the other hand, The Gift of Faith is miraculous in nature and produces supernatural signs and miracles. It is for believers only! It can only be received subsequent to salvation.

Saving faith is what Paul is describing in Romans 10:13-17 KJV. Notice, saving faith comes only through hearing the Word of God.

For whosoever shall call upon the name of the Lord shall be saved. How then shall they call on him in whom they have not believed? and how shall they believe in him of whom they have not heard? and how shall they hear without a preacher? And how shall they preach, except they be sent? As it is written, how beautiful are the feet of them that preach the gospel of peace, and bring glad tidings of good things! But they have not all obeyed the gospel. For Isaiah saith, Lord, who hath believed our report?" So, then faith comes by hearing, and hearing by the Word of God.

3. "The Fruit of Faith." "Faithfulness"

Saving Faith when developed becomes the Fruit of Faith. It can be found in Galatians 5:22, and is often translated "Faithfulness" (International Standard and the American Standard Versions). "But the fruit of the Spirit is love, joy, peace, longsuffering, kindness, goodness, faithfulness." The difference between Saving Faith and the Fruit of Faith is that Saving Faith has not yet gone through the process of sanctification. The children of God who have the Fruit of Faith believe God and are already assured of salvation. They have now taken their Saving Faith to the next level by believing God in such a way as to obey His commands. This is called sanctification and it is the developing process that produces faithfulness. "Even so faith, if it hath not works, is dead, being alone. Yea, a man may say, thou hast faith, and I have works: show me thy faith without thy works, and I will show thee my faith by my works" (James 2:17-18, KJV).

Incidentally, the Greek word used for "Faith" in Galatians' list of Fruits and the 1 Corinthians list of Gifts, is the same Greek word (pistis). Faith—the Fruit of the Sprit, found in Galatians 5:22, means faithfulness and refers to one's character, while Faith—the Gift of the Spirit, found in 1 Corinthians 12:9, refers to the supernatural act of believing.

Let me recap this section; Natural or General Faith is philosophical or psychological consent on a natural level. Saving Faith comes before salvation, and comes only through hearing the Word of God. Faith, the Fruit often called faithfulness, is produced after salvation by the process of sanctification. As Saving Faith is put through all the testing of a Christian's life, it is refined, and developed into the Fruit of Faith or Faithfulness. These tested and tried Christians have no more need for Saving Faith, because it is being refined and transformed into a daily walk of obedience and trust in the Almighty, a walk of Faithfulness (Galatians 5:22). These faithful Christians are already assured that they are God's child and Heaven is their home. Once Saving Faith is manifest, the writer of Hebrews encourages them to:

> "...draw near with a true heart in full assurance of faith, having our hearts sprinkled from an evil conscience and our bodies washed with pure water. Let us hold fast the confession of our hope without wavering [Faithfulness], for He who promised is faithful."
>
> Hebrews 10:22-23 ESV

Now that we have taken a close look at the other three types of faith seen in scripture, let's turn our attention to the third of the Power Gifts, the "Gift of Faith."

4. "The Gift of Faith" or as the Amplified Bible renders it "Wonder Working Faith."

Believers who have the Gift of Faith believe God in such a way that God honor their word as His own, and miraculously brings their word to pass. Jesus in Mark 11:23c, KJV states, "He shall have whatsoever he saith." The writer of 2 Kings 2:22 writes, "the water remains healed to this day, according to the word of Elisha which he spoke." James 5:17 reveals this truth in which he says, "Elijah was a man with a nature like ours, and he prayed earnestly that it would not rain; and it did not rain on the land for three years and six months." Finally, in Joshua 10:12, Joshua wrote, "Then Joshua spoke to the LORD in the day when the LORD delivered up the Amorites before the children of Israel, and he said in the sight of Israel, 'Sun, stand still over Gibeon; And Moon, in the Valley of Aijalon.'"

For the readers that might be thinking that the Gift of Faith closely resembles the Working of Miracles, we must stress that the Gift of Faith is very different from the Working of Miracles. Miracles are more active than passive; The Gift of Faith is more passive than active. Miracle power does things by the Spirit: The Gift of Faith receives things by the Spirit. For example, if Daniel when in the lion's den had slain the dreaded beasts with a gesture, it would have been the Gift of Miracles. In this particular case, however, Daniel absolutely knew that his fate was in God's hands, and by the Gift of Faith, he rested unharmed in the presence of the lions. The Working of Miracles was Daniel sleeping unharmed in the presence of the hungry lions. Whereas the Gift of "Wonder Working Faith," was the medium that enabled Daniel to receive the miracle and fall asleep unharmed in the midst of the hungry lions.

Another example is that of Shadrach, Meshach, and Abed-Nego in the midst of the burning fiery furnace found in Daniel. 3:13-18.

> Then Nebuchadnezzar, in rage and fury, gave the command to bring Shadrach, Meshach, and Abed-Nego. So, they brought these men before the king. Nebuchadnezzar spoke, saying to them, "Is it true, Shadrach, Meshach, and Abed-Nego that you do not serve my gods or worship the gold image which I have set up?" Now if you are ready at the

time you hear the sound of the horn, flute, harp, lyre, and psaltery, in symphony with all kinds of music, and you fall down, and worship the image which I have made, good! But if you do not worship, you shall be cast immediately into the midst of a burning fiery furnace. And who is the god who will deliver you from my hands?" Shadrach, Meshach, and Abed-Nego answered and said to the king, "O Nebuchadnezzar, we have no need to answer you in this matter." If that is the case, our God whom we serve is able to deliver us from the burning fiery furnace, and He will deliver us from your hand, O king. "But if not, let it be known to you, O king, that we do not serve your gods, nor will we worship the gold image which you have set up."

The Gift of Faith can be clearly seen in Shadrach, Meshach, and Abed-Nego's response to King Nebuchadnezzar.

"If that is the case, our God whom we serve is able to deliver us from the burning fiery furnace, and He will deliver us from your hand, O king. But if not, let it be known to you, O king, that we do not serve your gods, nor will we worship the gold image which you have set up."

Daniel 3:17-18

The Miracle can be seen in Daniel 3:25-26.

"Look!" he answered, "I see four men loose, walking in the midst of the fire; and they are not hurt, and the form of the fourth is like the Son of God." Then Nebuchadnezzar went near the mouth of the burning fiery furnace and spoke, saying,

"Shadrach, Meshach, and Abed-Nego, servants
of the Most High God, come out, and come here.'
Then Shadrach, Meshach, and Abed-Nego came
from the midst of the fire!

In summation, the Gift of Faith is a supernatural endowment by
the Spirit of God whereby anything spoken by God or His servant
will without hesitation or doubt come to pass. This supernatural
faith thereby produces immediate results in the form of miracles.
Its operation is one of a catalyst or a medium used to bring forth
a miracle.

The Gift of Faith listed in 1 Corinthians 12 is often erroneously
regarded as the basis of all other Gifts of the Spirit. Though it is
true that faith is needed to operate all the Gifts of the Spirit, it is
not true that the Gift of Faith is the one that operates them. In the
same way that all the Gifts are operated through faith, so is the
great Gift of Faith. Look at it this way: all motor cars and trucks
run on some type of gasoline, even the great eighteen wheelers
that carry the gasoline.

What is that faith that operates the Gifts, including the Gift of
Faith, and is the foundation to everything in the Christian life from
new birth to full redemption in His Glory? It is the development
of Saving Faith. Saving Faith can only come by hearing the Word
of God and is a gift from God (Romans 12), Saving Faith as a seed
saves, but when put through the process of sanctification becomes
the fruit of Faith or Faithfulness. When God takes this faithfulness
and empowers it above the believer's capacity to believe, it becomes
the Gift of Faith, which produces wonder working power.

Now before closing our discussion on the Gift of Faith, we
must once again consider some Scriptural uses of the Gift of Faith.

1. The Gift of Faith was employed for supernaturally blessing
    God's people by the use of human utterance.

A. Thus "By Faith" Isaac blessed Jacob concerning things to come (Hebrews 11:20, Genesis 27:28).

B. Balaam blessed Israel (Numbers 23:5~)

2. For personal protection in perilous circumstances.
   A. Daniel in the Lion's den (Daniel 6).
   B. Shadrach, Meshach, and AbedNego (Daniel 3).

3. For supernatural sustenance in famine or fasting.
   A. Widow of Zarephath in the midst of the famine (1 Kings 17).
   B. Elijah on a 4o day fast (1 Kings 19).
   C. Jesus on a 40 day fast (Matthew 4).

4. For receiving the astounding promises of God.
   A. Elijah's anointing to Elisha (2 Kings 2: 23-24).

5. For supernatural victory in a fight.
   A. Israel's victory over the Rephidims (Exodus 17:11).

6. To assist in domestic and industrial problems.
   A. A woman saving her sons from the creditors (2 Kings 4:17).

7. To raise the dead.
   A. A. Lazarus comes forth (John 11).
   B. Widow of Nain's son (Luke 7).

8. For casting out evil spirits.
   A. Deliverance by a prayersoaked handkerchief (Acts 19:12).
   B. Syro-Phoenician women's daughter (Mark 7:25-30).

Let me give one last example of the Gift of Faith; Smith Wigglesworth said "that if you will take a step of ordinary faith, when you come to the end of that faith, very often this supernatural gift of special faith will take over. One reason most people don't see the manifestation of special faith operating in their lives is that they don't first use what faith they already have."[20]

Under Smith Wigglesworth's ministry, at least three different people were raised from the dead; there were probably more. One instance of a person who was raised from the dead was a man named Mr. Mitchell, whom Wigglesworth personally knew.

> One day when coming home from an open-air meeting, Wigglesworth learned that his wife, Polly, was at Mr. Mitchell's house. The day before when Wigglesworth had visited Mr. Mitchell, the sick man had been close to death. As Wigglesworth hurried to Mr. Mitchell's house, he heard screaming coming from the house. On the way into Mr. Mitchell's room, he passed Mrs. Mitchell crying, "He's Gone! He's Gone!"
>
> Mr. Wigglesworth related his experience: "I just passed Mrs. Mitchell and went into the room, and immediately I saw that Mitchell had gone. I could not understand it, but I began to pray. My wife was always afraid that I would go too far, and she laid hold of me and said, "Don't Dad! Don't you see that he is dead?" But I continued praying. I got as far as I could with my own faith, and then God laid hold of me. Oh, it was such a laying hold that I could believe for anything. The faith of the Lord Jesus laid hold of me and a solid peace came into my heart. I shouted. "He lives? He lives! He lives!" And he is living today.[21]

Is it not time for the Body of Christ to start taking seriously the Gifts of the Spirit? Shouldn't we start earnestly seeking for their operation in the church? If the world and the church are not ready today to receive a man of God in which the Gifts are operating, we do not know of a time that the world or church will ever be ready. May all of us over the next few months and years, ask, seek, and knock for the manifestation of these Gifts in our lives. Remember Jesus said in Matthew 7:7-8, "Ask, and it will be given to you, seek, and you will find; knock, and it will be opened to you, for everyone who asks receives, and he who seeks finds, and to him who knocks it will be opened."

Chapter Questions To
Help Your Study

1. The second group of Spiritual Gifts is called the Power Gifts. Why?
2. The first is called the Gifts of Healings. True or False
3. What are some purposes for the Gifts of Healings?
4. The Gifts of Healings can be seen operating in several different ways, list three.
5. One essential element in ministering the Gifts of Healings is _____
6. Not everyone is given, the Gifts of Healings. True or False
7. What is Webster's definition of a miracle?
8. What are three other terms used to refer to miracles?
9. Give three divisions of miracles.
10. Give five uses of miracles.
11. What is the greatest of the three power gifts?
12. Give the Four kinds of faith.
13. Give some uses of the Gifts of Faith..

THE GIFT OF INSPIRATION

The third group of Spiritual Gifts is called, "The Gifts of Inspiration." This group, like the others, contain three different Gifts.

1. Prophecy
2. Divers Kinds of Tongues
3. Interpretation of Tongues

Prophecy

The Greek word "prophecy" (propheteia), is found in one form or another throughout the New Testament, and simply means to "speak for another." In the context of 1 Corinthians 12, it means one who speaks for God, His "spokesperson," or His "mouthpiece." It was and still is the declaration of those things, which by natural means cannot be known except by the mind of God. Prophecy is the name we give to the utterances God puts within us to reveal. The content of those utterances can be described as Words of Knowledge, or Words of Wisdom.

The general meaning of the most common Hebrew word for prophecy "Naba" is to "flow forth, or to bubble forth like a fountain."[22] Though much Old Testament prophecy was predictive (Ref. Micah 5:2), prophecy is not necessarily, nor even primarily predictive in nature nor is it prognostication or fortune telling. The Gift of Prophecy is "forth telling," which means to reveal or unveil. It is God by His grace revealing His will for mankind through a chosen and yielded vessel forth telling God's judgment and will for His people or for mankind in general. This judgment is based upon man's reaction to His Divine commands. That revelation can concern actions taken in the past, or present, and the results of those actions in the future. (For examples see Genesis 20:7, Deuteronomy 18:18, and Revelation 10:11, 11:3).

Prophecy, unlike Tongues, which is the supernatural utterance of the Holy Spirit in an unknown tongue., is the supernatural utterance of the Holy Spirit in a known tongue. Prophecy is not intended to open the future to idle curiosity; it is for a much higher purpose. It provides God's divine illumination to those whose faith needs confirming. Please carefully note what was just said. It provides God's divine illumination to those whose faith needs confirming. Anyone who has received the baptism in the Holy Ghost can be used to prophesy. God however, is the one who chooses whom He will use. "For ye may all prophesy one by one, that all may learn and all may be encouraged" (1 Corinthians 14:31 KJV).

When we look at such passages as 1 Corinthians 14:13, 24-25, we can easily see that the purpose of Prophecy is to edify, comfort, and encourage believers, while its effect upon unbelievers is to show that the secrets of a man's heart are known to God, to convict of sin and to move them to worship. Too often naive and unlearned Christians mistakenly look to prophecy for guidance. When prophecies are looked to in this manner they often lead to misunderstandings, mistakes, and often tragedy. At times, God uses prophecy to confirm what He has already revealed through His Word, or prayer to the Church or to an individual. This action edifies, comforts, and encourages the believer.

Human will and faith takes an active role in prophecy but not the human intellect. The proclamation, therefore, carries the same divine authority and power, no matter who delivers them. It matters not whether the proclaimer is a learned man or just a babe in Christ; it is God's divine authority and power using a willing and yielded individual. The operative word here is "using." God is "using" a vessel that He wills to use. God's decisions are not always what we consider the most logical. For example, look at Balaam's donkey; surely God could have made a better choice for a mouthpiece. Saints, we must not question God's choice of vessels. "'For My thoughts are not your thoughts, nor are your ways My ways,' says the LORD. 'For as the heavens are higher than the earth, so are My ways higher than your ways, And My thoughts than your thoughts'" (Isaiah 55:8-9). Again; the vessel God chooses is but a "mouthpiece" for the expression of God's divine Word, and is not to be questioned or judged. What is to be judged, however, is the prophecy itself? We are only to judge whether or not the content of that spoken word is in agreement with God's Word.

To gauge the importance of the Gift, a true studier of God's Word only has to notice that some form of the Greek word for "prophecy" (propheteia) occurs twentytwo times in 1 Corinthians 11-14. The frequency of the word suggests not only the importance of the Gift but the urgent need for its use. But just like any powerful tool its handling must be respected. Remember, Prophecy is entirely supernatural! For that reason, it should be used with extreme caution, "for the word of God is living and powerful, and sharper than any two edged sword, piercing even to the division of soul and spirit, and of joints and marrow, and is a discerner of the thoughts and intents of the heart" (Hebrews 4:12).

Many Christians have experienced, "false prophecies" or as one pastor friend of ours calls them "Prophelies," and have discovered that these "Prophelies" can be painful, misleading, and destructive. These Christians, more times than not are looking to God's "tool" for help, rather than to God Himself. True prophecy is a manifestation of the Spirit of God, and not of the human mind (1 Corinthians 12:7). It has no more to do with human powers of thought or reasoning than the healing of the man at the Gate Beautiful has to do with Peter and John's medical or surgical skills. It was supernatural in nature.

To examine more closely the Gift of Prophecy, we will now begin to examine four common errors surrounding it. Then we will look at six purposes for the Gift of Prophecy.

The Gift of Prophecy is the Same as the Prophetic Office.

This is probably the most common of all the errors. Although both the Spiritual Gift of Prophecy and the "Office of a Prophet" are called Gifts (Ephesians 4:8, 11; 1 Corinthians 12:28, 30), the "Gift of Prophecy" is given by the Holy Spirit to an individual (1 Corinthians 12, and 14), whereas the "Office" of a Prophet is given to the Church. It is also important to notice that both the holder of the "Gift of Prophecy" and the holder of the "Office of a "Prophet" are both called prophets (1 Samuel 10:10-14; Acts 21: 9-10). Yet there is a difference that can clearly be seen in Acts 21:9-10, where Philip's four daughters, "which did prophesy," are put in a deliberate contrast to "a certain "prophet" named Agabus. Who, being inspired by the Holy Ghost showed what would happen to Paul should he go to Jerusalem? Put simply, not everyone that prophesies hold the office of a Prophet, but everyone that holds the office of a Prophet, prophesies.

The Prophetic Office and the Gift of Prophecy are different for the following reasons:

1. The Office of a Prophet is a "position" prepared for an individual by God the Father for His universal Church, this position is of God's choosing (Mark 10:35-40). The person whom God places in that position cannot be separated from his appointed office (Ephesians 4:1), while the Gift of Prophecy is only an "instrument or tool" that can be used by many people (1 Corinthians 12:10). (We will study more on the office of a Prophet in a latter chapter.) Notice also, 1 Corinthians 14:1; in which Paul tells us to seek the "Gift" of Prophecy, not the "Office of a Prophet." Furthermore, the

Scriptures forbid us to seek after offices (Mark 10:35-40, James 3:1). While on the other hand, the Scriptures tell us to seek after Spiritual Gifts (1 Corinthians 14:1).

2. Although specific revelations of things outside the scope of God's Word (e.g. directions, warnings, events contained in the hidden past, present or future, etc.) were designed for correction and direction, and are necessary to the Prophetic Office, they are not necessarily included in the scope of the Spiritual Gift of Prophecy. 1 Corinthians 14:34 plainly limits the Gift of Prophecy to edification, exhortation, and comfort to men and speaking edification to the Church.

A. Also 1 Corinthians 14:5 compares the Gift of Prophecy with the Gift of Tongues plus Interpretation. This comparison suggests an exact correspondence in value between the Gift of Prophecy and the Gift of Tongues plus Interpretation. Also, nowhere in Scriptures is anyone who possesses the Gift of Tongues with Interpretation called a Prophet or a Seer.

The Gift of Prophecy is the Same as Prediction.

The Gift of Prophecy is not the power to predict the future. Notice 1 Corinthians 14:3, in which Paul states, "he who prophesies speaks edification and exhortation and comfort to men." lingers Bible dictionary defines prophecy as the oral or written message of the one prophesying.[23]

Don Basham in his book, Tongues, Interpretation, and Prophecy, defines prophecy this way, "Prophecy is speaking forth the message of God to His people."[24] He goes on to say that the message itself in many, if not most cases will not contain prediction about the future. Notice how the speaking forth and the message itself are separated. William Smith in his Bible Dictionary says, "It is certain that neither foreknowledge nor prediction is implied by the term in the Hebrew, Greek, or English language."[25] "Prophecy" simply means "one who speaks for another, a spokesperson, or a mouthpiece." Any revelation of future events (prediction) can only come through the Gift of the Word of Wisdom. A "Word of Wisdom" may be carried along with the prophecy and therefore the prophecy itself is mistaken as a prophetic utterance, but the Gift of prophecy simply is a gift that uses man as a tool that speaks what God has on His mind. The information contained within it can be classified as Words of Knowledge or Words of Wisdom, not the prophecy itself. To use a simple metaphor to clearly illustrate the differences, imagine the Gift of Prophecy being the microphone, in which God is speaking through, and what God is saying as a Word of Knowledge, or a Word of Wisdom.

Prophecy is Intended for Guidance.

Guidance is not indicated as one of Prophecies uses in the comprehensive definition in 1 Corinthians 14:3. It is not intended to replace common sense and natural judgment. Notice what the Psalmist says about guidance in Psalms 32:9a, "Do not be like the horse or like the mule, which has no understanding," or what the Lord Jesus Himself said in Luke 12:57, "Yes, and why, even of yourselves, do you not judge what is right?" Again, I reiterate what was said earlier, the Gift of Prophecy is not the power to predict the future. Notice again, 1 Corinthians 14:3 that defines prophecy's uses as "edification and exhortation and comfort to men." Not Guidance!

The Gift is the Same as Preaching.

The word for "preach" kerusso is a different word than the one used for "prophecy" propheteia. In Greek, there are many words translated "preach," none of which is prof-ate-yoo'-o, making preaching and prophesying totally different. The meanings of the Greek words translated "preach" are to proclaim, announce, or to cry out. So, what is to be proclaimed, announced, or cried out? The Gospel (Mark 16:15). Again, prophecy simply means to "speak for another," a "spokesperson," or a "mouthpiece." Prophesying is not preaching and preaching is not prophesying. In true preaching, the natural mind is operated by the Spirit. In prophesying, the mind of the Spirit is speaking through the natural speech organs of a believer. Preaching is divinely inspired, but not supernatural. Prophesying is every bit supernatural and fully inspired by God.

Listed below are six purposes for the Gift of Prophecy.

1. Prophecy is for God to speak to man supernaturally (1 Corinthians 14:3).
2. Prophecy is for the edification of the Church (1 Corinthians 14:3-4). The meaning of "edification" is to build up, spiritually, emotionally, and physically.
3. Prophecy is for the exhortation of the Church (1 Corinthians 14:3). The word "exhortation" in the original Greek signifies "a calling near, comfort, or encouragement." The Holy Ghost calls us to come near to the loving warmth of the Father's sweet presence. Does that not encourage us to do as Paul in 1 Corinthians 14:1 tells us to do? "Pursue love, and desire spiritual gifts, but especially that you may prophesy."
4. Prophecy is for the comforting of the Church (1 Corinthians 14:3, 31). The Greek word for "comforting" means "consolation, solace, comfort, in trial or distress. It's the same word that is rendered repeatedly "comfort" in 2 Corinthians 1:4. "Who comforts us in all our tribulation that we may be able to comfort those who are in any trouble, with the comfort with which we ourselves are comforted by God."
5. Prophecy aids in the learning of Spiritual matters (1 Corinthians 14:31). "For you can all prophesy one by one, that all may learn and all may be encouraged,"

6. Prophecy is used to convict the believer as well as the unbeliever and make manifest the secrets of the heart (1 Corinthians 14:22-25). Prophecy serves primarily the believers (verse 22), yet since it is understood by the mind it may serve also as a message straight from God to unbelievers as well (verses 24-25)

Closing this study on Prophecy, let's remind ourselves of these few scriptural facts.

1. We are expressly commanded to desire this Gift (1 Corinthians 14:1).
2. Prophecy is greater than Tongues when Tongues is not accompanied by Interpretation of Tongues (1 Corinthians 14:5). But Tongues and Interpretation of Tongues together are equal in value to Prophecy.
3. Prophecy is a manifestation of the Spirit of God (1 Corinthians 12:7, 11).
4. The Gift of Prophecy is not to replace the written Word of God, because only the written Word of God is infallible. Prophecy is to be judged for accuracy and fallibility, by the Word of God, and other prophets (1 Corinthians 12:7, 11, 13:8, 14:29; 1 Peter 1:25).
5. The possessor of the Gift is responsible for its use, misuse, suppression or control (1 Corinthians 14:29, 32-33, 40).
6. Finally, we must remember that the devil has a plan; it is cleverly conceived and fanatically executed, to destroy the supernatural aspect of worship. The supernatural aspect of worship frustrates and hinders his plans (1 John 4:4). Therefore, the focal point of his attack is our faith. If he can destroy our faith in the use of Spiritual Gifts, he can destroy the Gifts themselves. Timothy was warned against neglecting his Spiritual Gift (1 Timothy 4:14). He was exhorted to stir up the gifts within him, lest his ministry

be limited by fear, and the voice of the Spirit silenced through neglect (2 Timothy 1:1-7). That is what the devil wishes to accomplish.

Divers Kinds of Tongues

"Divers kinds of Tongues" is a supernatural utterance in an unknown tongue never learned by the speaker nor understood by the listener. Out of the nine Gifts of the Spirit discussed so far, seven of them are common to both the Old and New Testaments, while the remaining two Gifts have come into operation since Pentecost. These two are the most closely related of all the Gifts. They are "Tongues" and "Interpretation of Tongues."

We have already discussed in the chapter "Tongues in regard to the Baptism of the Holy Spirit" the personal nature of the Gift, and how the Gift benefited the believer. The three gifts that we are now studying however, Prophecy, Tongues, and Interpretation of Tongues are not personal, but they are designed for use in the meetings of believers. Keep in mind that the scriptural purpose of all the Gifts of the Spirit is edification, exhortation, and the perfecting of the entire body of believers (1st Corinthians 14:5, 12-13, 26).

In a person's private devotions, one can use Tongues in regards to the Baptism of the Holy Spirit to edify himself as freely as he wills. In public meetings, however, he must keep silent unless there is one present who possesses its complementary Gift, "Interpretation of Tongues." For by speaking in tongues without an interpreter, a man is speaking only to himself and God, and it does not benefit others in the body of Christ.

Therefore, let him who speaks in a tongue pray that he may interpret. For if I pray in a tongue, my spirit prays, but my understanding is unfruitful. What is the conclusion then? I will pray with the spirit, and I will also pray with the understanding.

I will sing with the spirit, and I will also sing with the understanding. Otherwise, if you bless with the spirit, how will he who occupies the place of the uninformed say Amen at your giving of thanks, since he does not understand what you say? For you indeed give thanks well, but the other is not edified. I thank my God I speak with tongues more than you all, let in the church I would rather speak five words with my, understanding, that I may teach others also, than ten thousand words in a tongue... But if there is no interpreter, let him keep silent in church, and let him speak to himself and to God (1 Corinthians 14:13-19, 28).

It is for this reason that our study must now turn to the complementary Gift to Tongues, "Interpretation of Tongues." These two Gifts when used together are (as stated earlier) for edification, exhortation, and the perfecting of the Body of Christ.

Interpretation of Tongues

Interpretation of Tongues is the supernatural showing forth by the Spirit of the meaning of an utterance in tongues not understood by the speaker or the hearers so that the Church, as well as the possessor of the Gift, may be edified (1 Corinthians 14:5). This interpretation does not come from the operation of the mind of the interpreter but from the mind of the Spirit of God. The interpreter does not understand the tongue he hears, but through the Spirit of God is interpreting what has been uttered into understandable speech. It is not his job to provide exact terms and phrases for the supernatural and unknown words he hears. A believer possessing the Gift of Interpretation of Tongues is not to pay attention to the tongues themselves because they are totally unknown. His only commission is to look to God for their meaning, in the same way that the speaker of the unknown tongue looks to God in full ignorance and total dependence, for what he should speak.

For one to fully understand this Gift, it is extremely important to examine the exact term used as its title. Please note that this Gift is entitled Interpretation of Tongues. It is not entitled Translation of Tongues and herein lies much of the misunderstandings and questions related to this Gift. The Greek word for interpretation is diermeneuo, which means "to explain thoroughly." It does not mean to translate. A "translation" is a rendering from one language to another in equivalent words or grammatical terms. An "interpretation" is a declaration of the meaning of the words used (1 Corinthians 14:11), and may be stated very differently than the precise structure and phrasing of the original tongue. The interpretation may come in different forms, for example pictorial, parabolic, descriptive, or literal. Only God and the interpreter's personality, back ground, and intelligence determines which.

For example, God's Word was translated from the original languages of Hebrew and Greek. In contrast, Joseph interpreted the Baker's and Butler's dreams by bringing forth their meanings (Genesis 40). Jesus gave an interpretation of the parable of the tares when he transposed the terms from the natural world to the spiritual world (Matthew 13:24-30 and 36-43). Let's use another example to further illustrate the difference. In Spanish the phrase "Dios es Amor," when translated into English is, "God is Love." But when a person is interpreting the phrase "Dios es Amor," he might say, "Our heavenly father, who we call Elohim or God Almighty, is the total personification of the perfect and pure expression and character of the indescribable affection He is."

Both the translation and the interpretation of the phrase "Dios es Amor" give us the meaning; however, one is an exact translation, the other an interpretation. The interpretation is different because it incorporates not only the meaning of the words, but the personality and character of the person interpreting.

In 1 Corinthians 14: 26-33 there are several observations and guidelines for the use of the Gift of Tongues and its interpretation that will help us to better understand its operation in the body of Christ.

1. God does not wish to silence those who speak with tongues, but wishes for them to enjoy greater freedom in the exercise of their God given Gift (1 Corinthians 14:27). That is why earlier in the chapter Paul instructs those who speak in other tongues to pray for the interpretation (1 Corinthians 14:13).

2. When the Gift of Tongues is in operation in the assembly, someone must interpret! The reason for this is given in 1 Corinthians 14:33a, in which Paul explains that, "God is not the author of confusion, but of peace." An unknown tongue with no interpretation can bring nothing but confusion.

3. There is a numerical limit of two or at most three placed on the Gift's operations (verse 29).

4. Each Gift is to be judged whether it be from God, by the body of believers (verse 29).

5. These Gifts are under the believer's control (verse 32).

These Spiritual Gifts brought with them problems. We see many of the same problems in the modern Church as well. It is prudent therefore, to examine the way the Apostle Paul addressed them. Many Corinthian believers were coming into service with the expressed purpose of speaking for God. It had become so bad that competition was taking place between believers over who could be used the most. These babes in Christ were, for pride sake, overusing and overlapping the Gifts to the point of disorder and even the destruction of the service. This was causing many unbelievers to leave and many unlearned believers to stumble. That is why Paul had to instruct them on their proper use.

How is it then, brethren? When ye come together,
every one of you hath a psalm, hath a doctrine, hath
a tongue, hath a revelation, hath an interpretation.
Let all things be done unto edifying. If any man
speaks in an unknown tongue, let it be by two, or
at the most by three, and that by course; and let
one interpret. But if there be no interpreter, let him
keep silence in the church; and let him speak to
himself, and to God.

1 Corinthians 14:26-28 (KJV)

The hurt and destruction caused by the misuse of these Gifts is why the apostle Paul in verses 27-28 gives straight forward and easy to understand instructions of their proper use. He instructs them that no more than two or three people should speak in tongues and then not altogether at one time but in succession, one after another. Even this was not to be done unless there was someone to interpret.

Let's look a little closer at the first of the guidelines. "Let all things be done unto edifying" (1 Corinthians 14:26b). How does everyone overusing, overlapping, and misusing the Gifts bring edification? It doesn't! Therefore, think outside yourself These Gifts were given for the edification of the whole body. We should use them in a manner that will uplift others. Then in verse 27 we are instructed that; "...if anyone speaks in a tongue, let there be two or at the most three, each in turn, and let one interpret." When a believer is operating in the Gift of speaking with other tongues, somebody must interpret! Notice the word one at the end of verse 27, it is not a numeral like the words two and three found in the same verse; it is a pronoun, which means "someone." It does not mean that the person who speaks with other tongues exclusively does the interpreting. For too often in our assemblies, that has been the case. This is wrong! If the person that speaks forth in tongues has the Gift of interpretation let him remain silent for a short time to allow others who are worshiping a chance to get involved "if anything be revealed to another that sits by, let the first hold his peace" (1 Corinthians 14:30, K.JV). If there is no interpretation after a short period of time, let him who spoke in tongues give the interpretation. If the giver of tongues does not have the Gift of Interpretation then let him keep silent unless he knows there is an interpreter in the congregation (verse 28).

For further clarification let us put verse 27, with verse 30, "if anyone speaks in a tongue, let there be two or at the most three, each in turn, and let one interpret...but if anything is revealed to another who sits by, let the first keep silent." By combining these verses, we see an affirmation of the purpose of this entire passage. Selfishness, pride, and the pursuit of prestige are to be avoided. Order and the edification of all is the objective.

In other words, although there may be two or three in the congregation who have the Gift of interpretation, each one should first defer to the other before interpreting. Beloved, keep in mind the three principles that run throughout this chapter. The first is that these spiritual gifts stem from love. Second, they are for the edification of believers and unbelievers, and third, "God is not the author of confusion, but of peace, as in all churches of the saints... Let all things be done decently and in order," (1 Corinthians 14:33, 40 KJV). To that end, let every believer blessed with these Gifts be fully aware of these three principles and act accordingly, so that the body of Christ will be edified, taught, exhorted, and comforted, most importantly is that Christ will be glorified in our lives and in our meetings.

In conclusion, giving a message in other tongues and interpreting it yourself is not unscriptural. However, the abundance of Scriptural evidence is on the side of corporate use not individual use of the spiritual ministry of the Gifts. Therefore brethren, if you are so richly blessed with the Gift of Tongues; wait before you interpret, think of others; first.

Chapter Questions To
Help Your Study

1. Prophecy, in its simplest form, is divinely inspired and anointed utterance. True or False

2. Prophecy is intended to furnish light to those whose faith needs confirming. True or False

3. The human will and faith is active in prophecy. True or False

4. Prophecy simply means what?

5. Name four common errors surrounding the Gift of Prophecy.

6. Preaching and Prophesying are totally distinct. True or False

7. Give the six purposes of the Gift of Prophecy.

8. The Gift of Prophecy is NOT to take the place of the written Word of God. True or False

9. The possessor of the Gifts is responsible for its

10. The Gift of Divers kinds of Tongues, or speaking with tongues is; the supernatural utterance by the Holy Spirit in languages never learned by the speaker and not understood by the hearer. True or False

11. The scriptural end of all the gifts of the Spirit found in 1 Corinthians 14 is for what?

THE ADMINISTRATIVE GIFTS

We will now begin our study of the "Administrative Gifts," or the "Fivefold Gifts of the Holy Spirit." They are often called the "Ascension Gifts." Because they were given after, the Lord ascended into the heavens and sat at the right hand of the Father (Ephesians I: 20, 4:10). Although they are not referred to as, the "Administrative Gifts," any where in Scripture, Bible scholars have christened them such. For the sake of this study, I will also use that designation. These Administrative Gifts were given to the Church Body, for the operation and fulfilling of God's ordained plan for His Body— the Church. In contrast, the Gifts of the Spirit were given exclusively to individual for edification, exhortation, and comfort.

These "Five-fold Gifts of the Holy Spirit" have also been called the "Hand" ministry gifts of the Church, or the "Hand" of the Body of Christ. The hand is the part of the Body of Christ that can reach out, and touch itself, and others. It is the part of the body that can clean, dress, feed, assist, support and direct. It can completely care for the body in all aspects of its character. These Gifts are like fingers. They can function as a finely tuned instrument that can accomplish the most extremely delicate of functions, like threading a needle for example, or it can function with the utmost strength and endurance, like grasping and holding on to great weights. Let's use this metaphor to help us understand the operation of each of these "Hand" ministries of the Body of Christ.

The Apostle has been likened to the thumb because unlike other fingers, it is opposable, in that it is the only digit on the human hand which is able to turn back against the other four fingers and thus enables the hand to refine its grip and to hold objects with superior strength which it would be unable to do otherwise. The opposable thumb has given the human race far superior physical and mental dexterity. It is also thought to have directly led to the development of tools.

This is also true of the apostles, in that the Apostle easily works in conjunction with other ministries. They are often needed to work with other ministries in order to accomplish the extremely hard task of saving a lost and dying world. Apostles make the Body of Christ aware of new areas, techniques, tools, and programs that can assist other ministries to better cope with problems found in different cultures around the world. The Apostle's ministry has given the Body of Christ added strength, intelligence, skill, expertise, wisdom, and ability far exceeding that of all the other ministries combined. The Body of Christ without the Apostle is as limited in its scope and function as a human hand without the thumb.

The index finger is likened to the Prophet because it is the pointing finger. The true Prophet's ministry always points the Body of Christ, whether that is the universal body or the local body, down the road God wishes it to go. That direction always leads God ward! The Prophet points out problems, dangers, detours, and even incomplete and unseen pathways that lie ahead. These insights give the Body of Christ the ability to function properly and efficiently without getting lost, wrecked, jammed up, or suffer loss of life. Just like an index finger pointing at a map, the Prophet points the Church at God's divine roadmap.

The middle finger which is generally the longest finger' is likened to the Evangelist because he has the longest outreach ministry. They truly are the architects of Acts 1:8. "But you shall receive power when the Holy Spirit has come upon you; and you shall be witnesses to Me in Jerusalem, and in all Judea and Samaria, and to the end of the earth."

The fourth finger or wedding ring finger is likened to the Pastor. The pastor's responsibility is to present the bride—the Church—chased, pure, and without spot or wrinkle to Christ when He returns. The wedding ring signifies soul ownership. The Church is Christ's, and it is solely His.

The shortest of all the fingers is the pinkie. A Teacher is likened unto the pinkie finger because a teacher has the shortest outreach of all the ministries. A teacher for the most part stays close to home. The pinkie finger is the only one of the fingers capable of reaching far into the ear in order to clear and open it, allowing the Word of life to be received easier. The teacher brings forth the instruction of the Word of God, and it is through hearing we develop and mature our faith. "Faith comes by hearing and hearing by the word of God" (Romans 10:17).

Whatever you prefer to call the Administrative Gifts or whether you agree or disagree with the metaphor given doesn't matter, as long as you understand they are Gifts. As Gifts, there is nothing we can do to earn them. We are either given them or we are not! In the case of all the Gifts of the Spirit, they are ours to use and steward according to the wishes of the Spirit. Also, since there are responsibilities that come with the Gifts, we must be aware that there is the potential for abuse or misuse.

Paul said in the opening verse of Ephesians 4, "I, therefore, the prisoner of the Lord, beseech you to walk worthy of the calling with which you were called" (Ephesians 4:1, emphasis added). Notice you were "called." "Called" simply means "invited." The same word is used referring to being called or invited in taking part in redemption, which Christ freely gave. Paul went on to say, "But to each one of us grace was given according to the measure of Christ's. Wherefore, He says: When He ascended on high, He led captivity captive, and gave gifts to men" (Verse 7-8).

Let me stress once again that these are Gifts; you are called or invited to possess. Moreover, according to Ephesians 4:1, we are also instructed to "walk worthy of that calling." Simply put this means we must live our lives in reverence and use our gifts with prudent care, godly fear, understanding and wisdom, not to misuse them for personal ungodly gain.

Please take notice of the exact wording used in Ephesians 4:11. "And He Himself gave some to be apostles, some prophets, some evangelists, and some pastors and teachers". There are four very important words in the beginning of this verse we must notice and understand. They are; "He Himself gave some." "He himself" refers to Jesus Himself, "gave"; not due to works, gender, color, or age, but He "gave" these Gifts according to His own will. He Himself gave only "some" these Gifts. Not everyone! In other words, Jesus freely, without any reward due to effort, invited us to take part in His calling and then He gave these Gifts to mankind. These Gifts were only given to some of His people, not to everyone. Everyone can and should be blessed by them, but not everyone possesses them.

According to Ephesians 4:11, the Administrative Gifts are: apostles, prophets, evangelists, pastors, and teachers. They should be appreciated and their benefits graciously accepted by everyone because they were given for a divine purpose. Their divine purpose is stated in the following verses.

For the equipping of the saints for the work of ministry, for the edifying of the body of Christ, till we all come to the unity of the faith and of the knowledge of the Son of God, to a perfect man, to the measure of the stature of the fullness of Christ, that we should no longer be children, tossed to and fro and carried about with every wind of doctrine, by the trickery of men, in the cunning craftiness of deceitful plotting, but, speaking the truth in love, may, grow up in all things into Him who is the head—Christ—from whom the whole body, joined and knit together by what every joint supplies, according to the effective working by

which every part does its share, causes growth of
the body for the edifying of itself in love.

Ephesians 4:12-16

Let me list all the aspects of the divine purpose for better
recognition.

1. Equipping of the saints for the work of the ministry.
2. Edifying of the body of Christ.
3. Unity of the faith is established.
4. Until we obtain the knowledge of the Son of God.
5. So we can, become perfect measuring up to the stature of Christ.
6. So we are, not tossed to and fro in our beliefs.
7. Until we speak the truth in love.
8. Until we grow, in all things into Him, Christ.
9. Growth and edification of the body of Christ in love.

APOSTLES

What is an Apostle? What is the role, ministry, burden, vision, and character of an Apostle? And finally, are there Apostles today?

First, we must come to grips with the understanding that God created us for fellowship with Himself. His ultimate goal is to dwell in the midst of His people (See Ezekiel 43:7-9; Zechariah 2;10-11). Our ultimate calling is to be a dwelling place for God!

> Now, therefore, you are no longer strangers and foreigners, but fellow citizens with the saints and members of the household of God, having been built on the foundation of the apostles and prophets, Jesus Christ Himself being the chief cornerstone, in whom the whole building, being fitted together, grows into a holy temple in the Lord, in whom you also are being built together for a dwelling place of God in the Spirit.
>
> Ephesians 2:19-22

Apostles "apostolos" in the Greek, simply means "one who is sent forth." They are given to the Church as master builders called and commissioned to help build the habitation of God. For a better understanding of the apostolic ministry, let's look at the apostle's main functions in the first century church. These main functions were:

1. To Preach the Gospel in unreached areas. Romans 15:20 says, "And so I have made it my aim to 'preach the gospel, not where Christ was named,' lest I should build on another man's foundation" (Emphasis added). This should be the Apostle's dominant passion.

2. Planting churches upon the foundation which is Christ. 1 Corinthians 3:10-11" According to the grace of God which was given to me, as a wise master builder I have laid the foundation, and another builds on it. But let each one take heed how he builds on it. For no other foundation can anyone lay than that which is laid, which is Jesus Christ." The apostolic ministry includes helping to establish churches that will stand fast in the truth of the Gospel around the world (Galatians 1:6-10, 3:1-3).

3. Appointing and training leaders once the Church is planted. Titus 1:5 "For this reason I left you in Crete, that you should set in order the things that are lacking, and appoint elders in every city as I commanded you." Paul says in Acts 14:21-23, And when they had preached the gospel to that city and made many disciples, they returned to Lystra, Iconium, and Antioch, strengthening the souls of the disciples, exhorting them to continue in the faith, and saying, "We must through many tribulations enter the kingdom of God." So, when they had appointed elders in every church, and prayed with fasting, they commended them to the Lord in whom they had believed.

4. Dealing with problems, false doctrines, or sins in the Church. The entire books of 1 and 2 Corinthians are an example of this apostolic function.

5. Promoting unity in the body of Christ. Refer to Ephesians 4:1-16, and Philippians 4:2. Besides dealing with developing unity in local assemblies, Paul also performed apostolic role of developing unity in the Universal Church (Acts 11:27-30; Romans 15:25-27; 1 Corinthians 16:14; 2 Corinthians 8-9).

6. Demonstrating and imparting the supernatural to all the saints. Acts 4:33 "And with great power the apostles gave witness to the resurrection of the Lord Jesus. And great grace was upon them all." Not only did the apostles show the power of God, but they also imparted it in special ways to other believers (Acts 8:4-20, 10:44-46, 19:16; 2 Timothy 1:6-7).

Although the first century apostles fulfilled these six general functions, the apostolic role was carried out quite uniquely by each of the apostles described in the New Testament; each one had his own special area of expertise. For example, Peter was particularly gifted at reaching the lost. Three thousand were saved after his first sermon. Paul seemed to excel in teaching and building believers in Christ's image. Paul was probably the greatest teacher other than Jesus that ever lived. Two thirds of the New Testament epistles are Paul's written teachings. John was an apostle with a prophetic heart. His passion was that God's people would walk righteously and in love relationships, both with the Lord and each other. James, the halfbrother of Jesus, also was recognized as an apostle (1 Corinthians 15:7), although his ministry was apparently more pastoral and primarily localized in Jerusalem.

Having an apostolic ministry does not automatically mean the apostle has the right to exercise full authority in all situations in every church. It was a ministry based on relationships and not just on calling. Paul told the Corinthians, "Am I not an apostle? Am I not free? Have I not seen Jesus Christ our Lord? Are you not my work in the Lord? If I am not an apostle to others, yet doubtless I am to You. For you are the seal of my apostleship in the Lord" (1 Corinthians 9:1-2).

It is also crucial to note that Paul's heart was not to establish a chain of "we are of Paul" churches, but to see each church function under the headship of Christ (Colossians 1:18; Acts 20:32; 2 Corinthians 11:2-3). The true apostolic vision, or ultimate goal if you will, is to see those who joined themselves to the Lord become Christlike in every aspect of their lives. Any true spiritual vision is not something that you decide is godly; the vision and calling must originate with God Himself. Notice how Paul describes his vision for himself and his spiritual children, "I have been crucified with Christ; it is no longer I who live, but Christ lives in me; and the life which I now live in the flesh I live by faith in the Son of God, who loved me and gave Himself for me" (Galatians 2:20). The prophet Haggai said it like this, "the latter glory of this house will be greater than the former" (Haggai 2:9). He did not say that the house was greater, but that the glory in it will be greater. This is why the Great Commission was not to make converts, but to make disciples. The burden is to make all the saints Christ centered not man centered. We as Christians must grasp the reality that the Lord does not exist for the Church; but the Church exists for the Lord. The more man centered or Church centered the Church becomes, the quicker she will fall into the prophesied apostasy.

The apostolic goal is not focused on the house as much as on the glory of the one who inhabits the house. The apostolic vision is Christcentered, not Churchcentered. Many people are drawn to church because of the beauty of the temple, the singing, the atmosphere, or the program and they never come to know Christ. Nevertheless, if men were led to Christ for the reality of the true significance of His atoning work they would inevitably end up in God's true Church. Ask yourself, what good is the most glorious temple in the world if the Lord is not in it? Whatever physical state your temple is in, would it not be more glorious if the Lord is there in all His glory and splendor?

Look at Paul's great apostolic prayer found in Ephesians 1:18-19.

> The eyes of your understanding being enlightened;
> that you may know what is the hope of His calling,
> what are the riches of the glory of His inheritance
> in the saints, and what is the exceeding greatness

of His power toward us who believe, according to
the working of His mighty power.

Paul does not pray that we will come to know anything that
is ours, only that we come to know what is His. This is truly the
apostolic vision and it perfectly reveals the character of a man with
the call of an apostle. Apostles are called to be the master builders
of God's dwelling place. If we therefore, look at the character each
master builder possessed we can easily recognize those called to
be apostles.

For example, of Moses, the first to build a dwelling place for
God, it was said:

> By faith Moses, when he became of age, refused to
> be called the son of Pharaoh's daughter, choosing
> rather to suffer affliction with the people of God
> than to enjoy the passing pleasures of sin, esteeming
> the reproach of Christ greater riches than the
> treasures in Egypt; for he looked to the reward.
>
> Hebrews 11:24-26

Moses chose to suffer affliction with the people of God,
esteeming the sufferings of Christ as greater riches than all the
treasures of Egypt. In like manner, Paul walked in continual
persecution, dangers, and setbacks, viewing all of them as a means
of greater authority and opportunity for the Gospel (Philippians 3).
Paul was a member of the aristocracy of the world's greatest empire,
yet he counted every title and privilege as "dung" (Philippians 3:8).

Paul's vision like Moses' had its foundation based on the
spiritual reward. It is often said that some people are so heavenly
minded that they are no earthly good. To some that may be true,
however, to the rest of them about whom this is said, they are the
ones who are suitable candidates for apostolic ministry. Are there
any men who have walked the earth since Jesus, who were more

heavenly minded than the apostles? An overwhelming problem in ministry today is that most ministers are too earthly minded to be of any spiritual good. "For he [Moses] endured as seeing him who is invisible" (Hebrews 11:27,). True spiritual vision demands that what we see with the eyes of faith, be more real than what we see with our natural eyes.

What about today? Are apostles needed today? Didn't the apostolic call end when the last of the original twelve died? These questions can best be answered by looking again at the list of functions of an apostle.

1. Penetrating unreached areas.
   There still are thousands of unreached people groups that, because of geographical or linguistic isolation, have never even heard of Jesus Christ.

2. Church planting and foundation laying.
   God anointed church planters are desperately needed in America and all over the world.

3. Appointing and training leaders once the church is planted.
   Whether or not our ministers attend a Bible college or seminary, today's young leaders are unlikely to receive the type of personal training and character development that Timothy received from Paul. Without a doubt, we are still in desperate need of true anointed spiritual fathers (1 Corinthians 4:14-17).

4. Addressing unresolved problems.
   We still need leaders able to courageously apply the Word of God to areas of sin, imbalance, false doctrine, and division.

5. Promoting unity.
   Unity is sorely needed in the Church today, and only those with apostolic insight and authority have the necessary gifts to bring it about in a significant way.

6. Demonstrating and imparting the supernatural.
   Today, more than ever, because of our society's increased interest in Satanism, the occult, and New Age practices,

the Church needs to be able to display and dispense the true power of God (1 Corinthians 2:4-5).

Let's examine one last thought regarding the questions. Are apostles needed today? And didn't the apostolic call end when the last of the original twelve died? We will respond to these questions with a question. What would you think if someone suggested that pastors, teachers and evangelists were no longer valid ministries of the church today? Wouldn't you think them off scripturally? Nevertheless, we often have allowed ourselves to be robbed of the ministries of apostles and prophets, because of false doctrines and beliefs. Remember apostles and prophets are found in the same list of ministries as pastors, teachers and evangelists (refer Ephesians 4:11).

We need more people functioning with apostolic and prophetic impact and fewer people worrying about having the titles: especially those individuals having or desiring the title without the calling or the Gift. Paul said it best when confronting this unrighteous desire, "Who then is Paul, and who is Apollos, but ministers through whom you believed, as the Lord gave to each one? I planted, Apollos watered, but God gave the increase. So then neither he who plants is anything nor he who waters, but God who gives the increase (1 Corinthians 3:5-7)."

Apostles like prophets, evangelists, pastors, and teachers are God's gift, God's calling, and God's work for God's ministry. We need to desire His fullness, reckoning ourselves as dead. Only then will the Church grow in Him. In God's kingdom, all authority comes from who you are in Christ, not your title. Your ministry is your function not your rank. In God's eyes, rank is earned by loving your neighbor as yourself, and serving God in absolute humility. The more we love others the greater our rank. A parishioner who loves more has a greater rank with God than the pastor who loves less. The moment we start looking at others in the reflection of our own pride, we become blind and deaf to the Spirit of God. Looking at the body of Christ through the eyes of humility will make you great in the kingdom of God (Matthew 23:11-12).

When we place our faith in Jesus as our Savior, He comes to live within us. Then He works to transform us, replacing our selfishness with Christ likeness. As we grow in grace and in our knowledge of God, our thoughts, words, and actions become more like our Lord's.

A.J. Gordon, the 19th century American minister, educator, and author, gave us an example of this process from nature.

> Two little saplings grew up side by side. Through the actions of the wind they crossed each other. By and by each became wounded by the friction. The sap began to mingle until one calm day they became attached. Then the stronger began to absorb the weaker. It became larger and larger, while the other withered and declined till it finally dropped away and disappeared. And now there are two trunks at the bottom and only one farther up. Death has taken away the one; life has triumphed in the other.[26]

Chapter Questions To
Help Your Study

1. What other name is used for the Administrative Gifts?
2. Three important words appear in Ephesians 4:11. What are they and what do they mean to you?
3. Name some things that the Administrative Gifts are given to accomplish, according to Ephesians 4:12-16.
4. What does the Greek word for Apostle mean?
5. Name four functions of an Apostle.
6. What is the true apostolic vision, or ultimate goal of an Apostle?
7. Spiritual vision requires that we see through the eyes of our _____

PROPHETS

And He Himself gave some to be apostles, some prophets, some evangelists, and some pastors and teachers.

Ephesians 4:11

The Greek word for Prophets is "Prophetes," which in Ephesians 4:11 is a Greek masculine noun. A masculine noun is one that identifies a specific person, one who is specifically called to speak forth or openly proclaim a divine message. This use of the masculine voice shows that these offices are for "some" or for "specific ones" to possess. They are not for everyone!

In the Septuagint, which is the Greek translation of the Old Testament Scriptures, a prophet is often referred to as a seer, it is the Hebrew word Roeh (1 Samuel 9:9). Roeh suggests that the prophet is one who has an intimate relationship with God, one who can see and touch God's heart. The Septuagint also translates the word Nabhi as prophet. This word means one in whom the message from God bubbles up or springs forth or one to whom anything can be secretly communicated. Therefore, the prophet is one upon whom the Spirit of God rests (Numbers 11:17-19), and also one to whom and through whom God speaks (Numbers 12:2; Amos 3:7-8).

A Prophet has a tremendous responsibility to speak God's message but only in divine truth. Divine truth must emanate out of the divine love of God's nature or it is not divine truth. Have no doubt that a prophet's message can originate from the Almighty and be presented in truth, but presented outside the loving expression of God's nature, and this truly divine message will go unheeded. If God's message is not delivered with the heart of God at the center, it will fail to become truth to those who hear it. Proverbs 13:17 (RV) says that "A wicked messenger falls into evil: but a faithful ambassador is health." The Revised Standard Version puts it this way. "A bad messenger plunges man into trouble, but a faithful envoy brings healing." A prophet needs to know more than what to say. He also needs to understand how to say it! No true prophet of God wants to use a hammer when a simple fly-swatter will do.

God also proclaims His messages in different ways. Look at Hebrews which says that "God, who at various times and in various ways spoke in time past to the fathers by the prophets" (Emphasis added). God most often speaks with gentleness and kindness (1 Kings 17:11-13), but sometimes He also speaks with discipline and rebuke (Numbers 20:11:12, Ezekiel 33:2-9). A prophet of God must know how to speak God's message as much as He knows what message to speak. He will be held just as accountable for what he says as how he says it (Jeremiah 23, Ezekiel 13).

Therefore, a prophet must be a man of prayer. It is only through constant prayer that a man of God can get the mind of Christ. A prophet must also be a man of the Word. He must be one that reads and rereads God's word. Knowing God's Word enables a prophet to use those parts of the Word that apply only to that given situation.

Prophets are given the right to express God's mercy as well as God's wrath. This is a weighty responsibility. A prophet must make sure he senses and follows exactly the Spirit's leading and to deny his own self. Much of what is revealed to a prophet can create havoc, fear, panic and unnecessary hardship if told improperly. Can you imagine what the results would be if a message was spoken to the wrong person or people or spoken when it was not meant to be spoken? For God often uses demonstrations, not words (Ezekiel 4,

Matthew 7:6), and sometimes God reveals His design to a person for the sole purpose of intercessory prayer (Genesis 18: 17~) To know exactly which God requires is the most grievous of all the Prophets responsibilities.

Another responsibility of a prophet is to make sure that the message is not deluded by sentiment. His anger, love, joy or sadness, or the wishes of the people can improperly affect a prophet's ability to hear the message and relate it properly. The prophet's emotions can affect the hearing of the message in its entirety, or the delivery of the message itself. It is seriously important therefore, for a prophet to adhere to the first Word God gives him. He should never change it or veer from it in any way due to sentiment.

There is a story in 1 Kings 13:11-23 about a young prophet who veered from God's first Word of instruction because another "man of God" encouraged him. Because of disobedience, the young prophet was killed by a lion. If the young prophet had only obeyed God's first orders, and not allowed the influence, courtesy, and kindness of the older prophet to influence him, the young prophet would not have died.

Simply put, but not so simply accomplished, a prophet must not alter, rationalize, or stray from the message God gives him. He should obey whatever God places upon him, and then let the mercy of the cross release his heart. If a prophet tries to alter the remedy God has deemed necessary to bring His children into maturity, it is sin! A prophet is simply a spokesman for God. He speaks what God tells him to speak the way God wants it spoken and to whom God wants it spoken. Nothing else! As Bob Mumford the founder and Director of "Life Changers" Inc. once said, "If we fix the fix God has fixed to fix us, God will only have to fix another fix to fix us."[27]

As well as being a spokesman or mouthpiece for God, the Old Testament Scriptures commonly call prophets "Watchmen." Being a watchman to the body of Christ is a significant characteristic of their ministry (Ezekiel 3:17, 33:7). The prophet was called a watchman because he functioned in the spiritual realm just as the earthly. watchmen did in the natural realm. Natural watchmen were stationed at specific posts on the walls of the city. This position gave them the visibility to watch for the king or other members of nobility to announce their coming. They were also to look for enemies from, without or disorder arising from within the city, or camp. These watchmen were especially trained to be able to distinguish the enemy from their brethren.

Prophets are men and women of God who mainly operated in the spiritual realm They are called and trained by God for several purposes. They are to recognize the enemy, his ways, his deceptions, and recognize the enemy, to boldly proclaim what God intends for His people. Then he is to direct God's people in the direction often called the "straight and narrow road that leads to life" (Matthew 7:13). His authority, which is God given does, have its limits.

> Prophets were not the elders at the gates, nor did they have the authority to open or close the gates of a city, neither did they have the authority to mobilize the militia against the enemy. Their job was to communicate what they saw to those who had that authority That is why they could not be overly prone to sound the alarm or to request that the gates be opened. They had to be accurate in their discernment, because if there were too many false alarms the people would begin to disregard them. If they were careless and let an enemy through the gate, they could jeopardize the entire city. Therefore, this was an extremely crucial position for which accuracy and dependability was essential and required of the prophets.[28]

The Prophet's ministry has been given to the Church, but it can only function properly if it is correctly related to the other ministries

(Ephesians 4:11). All these ministries are still being restored to their true biblical place. The watchman's ministry cannot function properly until the other ministries have taken their proper place first. Therefore, it is our duty as members of the Body of Christ to find our God appointed places, and position ourselves there. This will bring order and blessings to the Body of Christ, increasing its power and authority accordingly.

The Biblical positions of the watchmen in the Old Testament were.

1. On the walls of the city (Isaiah 62:6-7).
2. Walking about in the city (Song of Solomon 3:3).
3. On the hills or countryside (Jeremiah 31:6).

If we look at these positions and relate them to the Body of Christ and the Church, they will provide us with a practical picture of the operation of the Prophets ministry.

Prophets who were placed on the walls of the city had an elevated perspective. That position enables them to see both outside and inside the city. These men were trained to recognize both the enemy and their brethren from great distances, though they had no authority to confront either. They simply gave their information to the elders who sat in the gates. Only the elders of the city had the authority to command the gates opened or closed and to sound the alarm.

The watchman appointed to walk about inside the city could observe activity within the walls more intimately. These were specifically trained to make a way for the king or the nobility who were passing through or to recognize and confront disorder or unlawful behavior. They could apprehend violators, but they could not impose sentences. Sentences also came from the elders.

The watchmen on the hills patrolled the borders and countryside. They could see either the enemy or nobility long before they arrived in the city. They, too, were specially trained to distinguish their countrymen from foreigners or from their enemies who came as traders or ambassadors, These Watchmen like the others did not have the authority to call for a mobilization of the defenses or to let foreigners freely pass. Their job was only to communicate what they saw to the elders who were the only ones that had such authority.

In Revelation 21:2, the bride of the Lamb is referred to as a city. Therefore, relating that to the position of watchmen, the "city" would be indicative of the church, including either a local congregation or the Church universal. The Lord has called individuals whose main function is to be a watchman in each of these three places in and around the Church. He has some whose only purpose is to be watching within the Church for the movement of the King, to make a way for Him, and to recognize and report disorder, or unlawful behavior to the elders. There are some who have been given such a place of vision that they can see both inside and outside the city. There are also watchmen whose main calling is to roam around as scouts in the world. They are the ones who look out for false teachers and teachings, heretical doctrines, cults, new and old, on the horizon or rising up in the midst of the sheep. They are there to detect persecution before it breaks out against the body of Christ, or even wolves in the midst of God's people.[29]

Isaiah 62:6-7 states that the function of the watchman is to pray and to guard. This is crucial to understand because most discernment will come through prayer. In Ezekiel 3:17, the watchmen were to hear from the Lord and only warn the people. This is where many who are called as watchmen depart from their course. Their downfall begins when they begin looking for the enemy more than they look to the Lord. Both their vision and discernment then become distorted. Remember the watchman's ministry is a spiritual one. True spiritual vision is in the spiritual realm. The spiritual realm is entered only through much prayer, fasting and worship. The first principle of this ministry is that more than looking for the enemy; the watchman must be in constant communication with the Lord.

Jeremiah 6:17; Isaiah 21:5-10 and Habakkuk 2:1-3 address this aspect of the watchman's ministry.

One of the basic functions of the Prophetic ministry, which is often overlooked but is desperately needed, is to "know the times in which they live" (Isaiah 21:11-12). Therefore, as we proceed toward the end of this age, timing will become increasingly critical in all that we do. We must pray for the Lord to raise up in the last day "of the sons of Issachar who had understanding of the times, to know what Israel ought to do, their chiefs were two hundred; and all their brethren were at their command" (1 Chronicles 12:32).

Dear Lord, help us to recognize the times and the seasons, and be prepared for what we are shown, Amen!

Asaph, who was one of the psalmists, in one of his most desperate lamentations for Israel his under siege nation wrote, "We do not see our signs; There is no longer any prophet; nor is there any among us who knows how long" (Psalm 74:9). The Lord wants His people to know when He is going to move, when judgment is coming, and when the enemy will come. God declares this truth in Amos 3:7, "Surely the Lord GOD will do nothing, unless He reveals His secret to His servants the prophets." This is an essential aspect of the prophetic ministry that must be recovered and repositioned correctly in the Body of Christ. If not, we will continue to pay for it with unnecessary defeats and catastrophes.

We would do well to ask the same question that Job asked, "Since times are not hidden from the Almighty, why do those who know Him see not His days [timing] (Job 24:1). If one reads the rest of Job 24, it is almost a commentary on the present condition of much of the Body of Christ. When we fail to recognize the timing of the Lord, even our spiritual guidelines and boundaries become blurred.

Pastors and elders will never function on the level of authority in which they are called; until the watchmen takes the burdens upon themselves that they have been called to carry. Until a scriptural relationship between leaders and watchmen is established, the watchmen cannot function properly, and our leaders will continue to be needlessly blindsided by the enemy.

Paul talked about how careful he was to stay within the realm of authority that had been appointed to him (2 Corinthians 10:12-14). He knew that if he positioned himself outside the limits that God had set for him, he would be vulnerable to the enemy. He also knew that the Church that includes babies as well as mature saints would also be in grave danger, because they could receive wrong direction and leadership unless they were under the watchful eyes of a true prophet of God. Let the Church of God be aware of these two most important safety measures. First, leaders must learn to let the watchmen do what they are called to do. Second, watchman must learn that it is their job to simply transmit information, not to dictate policy.

One last thing about Prophets, a watchman who is appointed to patrol out in the world (researching cults, political or philosophical trends, etc.) will become a stumbling block if he tries to watch what is going on in the Church, for that is outside his realm of authority. Similarly, those who are given to watch over the Church can develop paranoia if they start watching what is going on in the world. it is hard for watchmen to stay within their realm of authority, but it is absolutely necessary that they do just that. When they do not, the consequences will usually be negative.

Finally, it is a dangerous thing for us to exalt these messengers beyond the place where God has placed them. On the other hand, it is also dangerous for us not to recognize the authority that God has given to them. This exaltation or non-recognition may cause us not to receive the messenger or the message the prophet is carrying from of the Lord.

The foolishness of Ananias and Sapphira was that they failed to recognize what authority was working in Peter (Acts 5:1-12). Peter was no longer just a fisherman; he was a vessel filled with the Holy Spirit. That lack of recognition led to a lie that caused them to be judged. Realize also that Ananias and Sapphira were not punished by the believers or the elders. They were killed by God! The Bible says that great fear fell on the Church because of the divine judgment God brought upon them. Dear Lord, let us have reverential fear because of your mercy, not because of your judgment.

Today, ministers have fallen to what may be an alltime low in the esteem of the world. This could be a deadly trap when the Lord again raises men of true apostolic and prophetic authority. The greater the light one has, the greater the judgment that will come upon him (Luke 12:48). When we honor the Lord's messengers, we are not unduly honoring men. We are, however, honoring the Lord. Just as the honor that we give to a country's ambassador reflects the respect that we have for his government, so does the honor we show God's ambassadors. If we allow the darkness of cynicism that prevails in the world today to influence the Church, we will pay a terrible price when the Lord reveals His servants or Himself.

Beloved, the best is yet to come. What we are about to see cannot be credited to man. No amount of money or special promotions can make it happen. The Lord is going to anoint people in these last days placing them in their proper positions unifying the corporate body to work like a well-oiled machine with each well-positioned part working in humility and power. These parts will yield to one another so the Lord can have his way in His Church and in His people. Only then will we see the kind of authority and power in which Elijah walked. We will see the kind of victory that Elijah saw over the false prophets and false Gods. Only then will we see a returning of the hearts of the fathers to the children and the children to the fathers. And only then will we also see a great spiritual generation depart to be with the Lord. They will go in glory and leave a generation behind that has twice as much power, and authority as they did, but only if we truly desire it (2 Kings 2:9).

There is a spiritual principle through which spiritual authority passes. This principle is found through the humility to honor those to whom honor is due. We must see the Lord's authority in those He has appointed, even when they do not meet our human expectations. Our relationship to that principle determines how much authority we can be trusted with. Our obedience to that principle will determine how much fruit we will leave behind. Finding and flowing in God's divine principle is therefore imperative for those who would serve the purpose of God in their generation.

May God show us those whom He has ordained to be servants on our behalf. Open our ear's dear Lord to listen, our hearts to hear, and our wills to obey, in Jesus' name, Amen!

Chapter Questions To Help Your Study

1. The Greek word for Prophet means what?
2. What is another commonly used Old Testament name for Prophets?
3. What are the three biblical stations a Prophet occupies?
4. Give the advantage each Prophet's station would have over the others.
5. What is the bride called in Revelation 21:2?
6. According to Isaiah 62:6-7 what was the function of the watchmen or Prophet?
7. What one basic function of a Prophet is overlooked but is still desperately needed?
8. What is the Prophet's job when they spiritually see something?
9. What is not the Prophet's job when they spiritually see something?

EVANGELISTS

I will build my church, and the powers of hell will
not conquer it.

Matthew 16:18 ISV

We will now continue our study on the Administrative Gifts with a look at evangelists, the third gift listed in Ephesians 4:11. And He Himself gave some to be apostles, some prophets, some evangelists, and some pastors and teachers", The Greek word for Evangelist is euaggelistes, which means preacher or messenger of the Good News (Gospel). Missionaries are also considered evangelists because they are preachers of the Gospel. The term missionaries came to be used in the early Church as the designation of a special class of evangelists because they usually go into areas that had not heard the Gospel.

Never in the history of the world has it been more evident that Jesus is building His Church. In Africa, the Christian church is growing thirtytwo times faster than the birth rate. In Korea, the Christian church is growing four times faster than the population increase. Currently, over 70% of Americans believe that they have had a born-again experience with God. Karl Marx wrote, "Philosophers have only interpreted the world differently; the point is however, to change it."[30] This is the calling of the Evangelists. This fact, is grounded in the truth of the Gospel "that God was in Christ, reconciling the world to Himself " (2 Corinthians 5:19), and this is what makes evangelism an absolute necessity.

Jesus' method of reaching the world was always a few special selected and ordained men, going forth in the power of their calling to reach the unreached. It started by Jesus' selection of only twelve out of the multitudes that followed Him. Please understand Jesus is not interested in numbers or the best laid plans of men. He is looking for men and women who will follow after Him with a pure heart of faith. Jesus started to call these special individuals before He ever preached a sermon. He kept these men close to Him until He felt they were ready to minister and then He filled them with power and sent them forth two by two. The church is called to be a witness, but these selected men were called to witness. Do not take this the wrong way. We are all told to bring forth the Gospel of Christ. We are to be a living epistle by living a godly life (2 Corinthians 3:2) along with written and verbal speech. Our lives, once yielded to the Holy Spirit will always have opportunities to be witnesses and bring forth the Gospel.

It is the evangelist however, who is not only called to be a witness but also to witness. He is empowered and then sent forth to the far corners of the world to bring forth the good news of salvation to a lost and dying world. Once salvation has been accepted, the new believer's instruction and pastoral care fall under the calling of the pastors and teachers.

The calling to be an evangelist does not come out of a godly life alone, though it does play a major part. It does come, however, out of a God ordained calling and empowerment to do that one specific job. Keep in mind that the evangelist without the church's backing is as useless as a powerful war ship without fuel. The fuel must be supplied by the church; it gets the evangelist to the place where he can fire the unstoppable omnipotent Word of God (Isaiah 55:11). If the church fails to support the evangelists, this powerful war ship is set adrift and is rendered useless.

Ephesians 4:11 places the evangelist in the center of the other four Administrative Gifts. This God ordained placement lead many to surmise that evangelists should be standing between the two other groups. Evangelists are sent forth as missionary preachers of the Gospel by the first group (Apostles and Prophets), and as such they prepare the way for the labors of the second group (Pastors and Teachers).

The evangelists were ordained ministers (2 Timothy 1:6), whom the apostles took for their companions in travel (Galatians 2:1), and sent them out to settle and establish such churches as the apostles themselves had planted (Acts 19:22). They were not fixed to any one particular place; they were only to continue there until they were recalled (2 Timothy 4:9). We can draw this same conclusion in the case of Paul and Agabus going to see Philip (Acts 21:8-10). Other administrators can do the work of evangelists as well. They might even claim the title of an evangelist (Acts 8:25, 14:7; 1 Corinthians 1:17). But they are not called or empowered to be evangelists. The calling of the evangelist is to proclaim the Good News of salvation to those who have never heard it.

Take note for a moment the statement above—the calling of the evangelist is to proclaim the Good News of salvation to those who have never heard it. It is this teacher's conviction that an evangelist is not a person who goes from church to church holding revivals. An evangelist is one that is called to a people who have not yet heard the Good News. Those people are on the street, or on some mission field, they are not in the Church. Do not misunderstand, there are some unsaved souls that find their way into a pew and should receive ministry, that falls under the authority of the Pastor's ministry. An evangelist by calling is one who goes to the unchurched. He is not one who goes church to church holding revivals for weeks and months at a time. Revival by definition is returning life to someone that has had life before, not to those that have never been alive before; in other words, revivals are for the Body of Christ not for the unsaved. This takes the revival ministry out of the hands of an evangelist, where it does not belong, and places it squarely in the hands of the other administrators.

An evangelist can if necessary, spend weeks and months in a church in order to establish it. Immediately upon that establishing, he must turn over the Pastoring and teaching of the new saints to those who are called to those ministries. He must then go and minister to those who have not heard the Gospel once again.

Let's now look at some qualifications which are needed to be an evangelist. We will do this by examining the life and ministry of Philip, one of the first ordained evangelistic deacons in the Word of God. This Philip is not the apostle Jesus called; whose brother was Nathaniel (John 1:43-45). Philip the evangelist was ordained a deacon in Acts 6:5. We know nothing of his family ancestry. As a deacon, we first read of Philip at his appointment. His name follows Stephen on the list given in Acts 6:5. After the death of Stephen in Acts 7, Philip went to the city of Samaria, carrying the Gospel with him. He was first called an evangelist in Acts 21:8, when Paul and his company stayed at Philip's home in Caesarea.

Philip the Evangelist was a Man who was broad minded. He was not a man with a singletrack mind who could not change or be moved by the movement of the Spirit. "Then Philip went down to the city of Samaria and preached Christ to them" (Acts 8:5). Remember how despised the Samaritans were by the Jews. No Jew would ever be caught dead speaking with a Samaritan (John 4:9). While there, he did many great miracles and brought salvation to many.

Philip was also a Man Led of the Spirit. Let's look at Acts 8:26-30.

> Now an angel of the Lord spoke to Philip, saying, "Arise and go toward the south along the road which goes down from Jerusalem to Gaza, which is desert," so he arose and went. And behold, a man of Ethiopia, a eunuch of great authority

under Candace the queen of the Ethiopians, who had charge of all her treasury, and had come to Jerusalem to worship, was returning. And sitting in his chariot, he was reading Isaiah the prophet. Then the Spirit said to Philip, "Go near and overtake this chariot." So, Philip ran to him, and heard him reading the prophet Isaiah, and said, "Do you understand what you are reading?

An evangelist is not afraid to go where he is led, even though the directions are without explanation and the way treacherous.

Philip was a Man who was Willing to Learn. Jesus selected men, for the most part, who were "unlearned and ignorant" according to the world's standards" (Acts 4:13), Men Jesus knew to be teachable, Philip did not understand or accept what had happened to Jesus and what was then happening to the Church. Remember he fled from the persecution of Saul. God, however, sees the heart of man. At the beginning, Philip's heart was weak, his understanding limited, but God saw the pureness of his heart and his teachable spirit, and therefore, God used him.

Philip was a Man who Preached Nothing but the Complete and Pure Gospel

So, the eunuch answered Philip and said, I ask you, of whom does the prophet say this, of himself or of some other man?" Then Philip opened his mouth, and beginning at this Scripture, preached Jesus to him. Now as they went down the road, they came to some water.

And the eunuch said, "See, here is water what hinders me from being baptized?" Then Philip

> said, "If you believe with all your heart, you may."
> And he answered and said, "I believe that Jesus
> Christ is the Son of God.
>
> Acts 8:34-40,

The Gospel is defined for us in 1 Corinthians 15:1-4 as, "how that Christ died for our sins according to the scriptures; and that He was buried, and that He rose again the third day according to the scriptures." Evangelists especially, should strictly adhere to this definition. When we start to cater our messages to the crowd, we become nothing more than a peddler on the side of the road selling magical elixir. Evangelists are called to preach nothing but the complete, uncompromised, pure, living Word of God and Christ crucified. If you need an example of what is being said, look at Rev. Billy Graham. His messages are simply stated, precise, and to the point. They define sin. They show you the consequences of that sin. They are always encompassed by the cross. He shows you the way to Christ's forgiveness and invites you to accept His atoning work. He is truly a God called and ordained Evangelist. He is a man who knows his calling and without compromise walks therein.

One last thing can be noticed about Philip the evangelist. Phillip was a man who had a godly household. Philip's and his family's lifestyle were a portrait of his faith.

> On the next day we who were Paul's companions
> departed and came to Caesarea, and entered the
> house of Philip the evangelist, who was one of the
> seven, and stayed with him. Now this man had
> four virgin daughters who prophesied.
>
> Acts 21:8-9

Philip had four virgin daughters all of which knew the Lord, all four in the ministry, all possessing the Gift of Prophesy. Philip's home was a haven of rest to those who were tired, weary, and in need of a safe place to lay their heads.

Tradition is conflicted and uncertain about the later life of Philip. The Greeks record that Philip became the Bishop of Tralles, in Lydia, but the Latins say he ended his days in Caesarea. Whichever is the case, tradition and history hold him up as a great man of faith, an Evangelist mightily used of God to enhance God's kingdom on earth.

Let's discuss for a moment the distinct difference between evangelizing and an Evangelist. According to Isaiah 43:10, Matthew 10:7, 28:19-20, Mark 16:15; Luke 9:2, 60, 24:46-49, John 15:27, Acts 1:8, 5:20, 8:4, 2 Timothy 4:2 and others, we are commanded to evangelize. All born again believers will "receive power when the Holy Spirit has come upon them; and they shall be witnesses to Me in Jerusalem [their home town], and in all Judea [their state], and Samaria [their country], and to the uttermost parts of the earth" (Acts 1:8). Not everyone who evangelizes has the special gift of being an Evangelist. God especially gives some to be Evangelists (Ephesians 4:11).

Although God gives some to be Evangelists for the sole purpose of winning the lost, we are not to believe that they are the only ones that can and should evangelize. So successful has Satan been with this deception that it has been estimated that probably ninety five percent of American church members have never led anyone to Christ. Thus, the army of Christ has been more than decimated, and the response from the pew has for the most part been, "Let the clergy do it." Remember over ninety nine percent of the Church is made up of laymen. Because the laity for the most part is AWOL, there is little doubt that the battle for the souls of men is being lost.

God commands everyone to witness the Gospel. Reports that have come forth from many pastors and evangelists from around the world are that the most significant factor in generating the growth of the Church is the mobilizing of the laity[31].' Increasingly, Christians worldwide are being energized by God, and they are now realizing that the Great Commission has been given to the entire Church for evangelizing not just the clergy.

Evangelists are truly blessed, called, and gifted men of God. These special men and women should be respected as much as and even more than the others in the list of Ephesians 4:11. These men and women must daily go where no man has gone before, with the Gospel. Often, these individuals go right into the heart of enemy territory, territory where physical and spiritual dangers abound. They go into areas where the Holy Spirit has never been invited. They go where they are unwanted and hated. But still they go! They go girded only by their faith and trust in their calling. Unlike apostles and pastors, these men often go without the daily prayers and monetary support necessary to fight such a spiritually brutal and savage war. This must change. The church must wake up to the importance of these special men of God!

Some time ago, I was having a lengthy discussion with a pastor of a small church in the Bronx. This Pastor is a member of a major Pentecostal denomination. He said some things that were very interesting. I would like to share them with you. Our discussion centered on the Administrative Gifts. He said that he believed that God was reestablishing them today in our churches. However, he was seeing a dramatic drop in the number of Evangelists going forth, when I asked him why, his response was startling. He said, "Most of the ones who formerly were going forth evangelizing throughout the world, were being destroyed for a lack of support. This lack of support was coming from both the clergy and the laity They are going into unknown areas with an annual income around twelve thousand dollars." He continued by saying that he felt that this was the reason most evangelists were going from church to church, running revivals instead of going to the unreached areas of the world, and that he feared for the repercussions that this lackadaisical attitude on the part of the clergy and laity was having on the Church. This brother was greatly bothered by the Church's lack of involvement in evangelistic ministries. It bothered him so much that he began getting a group of pastors together to discuss this problem.

Many of us go to churches that have no ongoing evangelistic ministry or even an adequate fund for evangelistic outreach. Our pastors are doing all the work of evangelism by home visitations, hospital visits, or even going to community meetings, and that is the extent of any evangelism in the church. However, this is not the sole and exclusive job of a pastor. Elders and laity should be doing this job along with the pastor.

Somewhere in most churches, there is a track rack. Most of the time however, these racks are empty, or they are partially filled with worn out, out dated, and out of style tracts, many of which haven't been touched in some time. Think back, when was the last time anyone made an emotional appeal to the congregation to take the tracts and hand them out to the unchurched? When was the last time someone in your church appealed to the congregation on behalf of an evangelist? How long has it been since someone from the church headquarters came to petition for funds for an evangelistic service? Granted many churches have some kind of missionary fund or a special missionary offering, which is used to support a church sponsored missionary. But how often do we support evangelism local or worldwide in the same way?

When was the last time you led someone to the Lord? When was the last class on evangelism in your church? When was the last time you invited anyone who did not know the Lord to an evangelistic meeting? When was the last time you ever invited people to your home for the explicit purpose of telling them about Christ? If you gauge yourself by your responses, don't you think that what this dear brother was saying about lack of support is very true? What do you think God's attitude is regarding the lackadaisical attitude of the clergy and laity toward evangelism? What do you think His reaction will be in response to that attitude?

Tony Campolo, the author of "Hot Potatoes Christians Are Afraid to Touch," writes.

> On a number of occasions, I have taken an informal survey to see how people have come to know Jesus. I ask how many people became Christians as the result of listening to some Christian radio show.

Seldom does a hand go up. When I ask how many were saved through a Christian television show, the response is not much better. Out of a crowd of several thousand people, usually just a few hands go up when I ask how many have become Christians because of a sermon they heard. Usually only two or three percent of the crowd responds. But when I ask how many have become Christians because some person loved them and shared the gospel with them, the response is always overwhelming. There is never any doubt after such surveys that the best and most "powerful" means of evangelism is not TV at all. But ordinary people who love their friends and relatives enough to tell them about Christ.[32]

Evangelism is the crucial component God created for the salvation of mankind. It is also essential for the growth of the Church. Evangelism will not be easy, nor must it be a onetime effort. Evangelism must be an ongoing continual effort of Christians. This effort however, will be a physical, emotional, and spiritual war that must be fought on three fronts.

The First Front is Prayer.

Without the effectual fervent prayers of the righteous, nothing can happen. The spirit of man cannot be broken or his will changed on the physical plane. The apostle Paul put it this way; "The natural man does not receive the things of the Spirit of God, for they are foolishness to him; nor can he know them, because they are spiritually discerned" (2 Corinthians 2:14)." Only God through the drawing and life changing power of the Holy Spirit can break a man's spirit. He then replaces the sinful heart of man with a pure heart, a heart that is after God. But this can only happen if we pray. Our prayers should be both intercessory and militaristic in nature.

The Second Front is Physical.

Paul writes to the church of Corinth that, "You are our epistle written in our hearts, known and read by all men" (2 Corinthians 3:2). We are Christians; we are to be Christlike. We are to be an example of light and a preservative to a dark and decaying world. Remember what Paul said to the Philippians, "Brethren, join in following my example, and note those who so walk, as you have us for a pattern" (Philippians 3:17). To the Thessalonians, Paul wrote, "Not because we do not have authority, but to make ourselves an example of how you should follow us" (2 Thessalonians 3:9). Finally, let us look at Paul's command to Timothy, a young pastor in Ephesus. "Let no one despise your youth, but be an example to the believers in word, in conduct, in love, in spirit, in faith, in purity" (2 Timothy 4:12).

The Third Front is Verbal.

> How then shall they call on Him in whom they have not believed? And how shall they believe in Him of whom they have not heard? And how shall they hear without a preacher? And how shall they preach unless they are sent? As it is written: "How beautiful are the feet of those who preach the gospel of peace, who brings glad tidings of good things!" But they have not all obeyed the gospel. For Isaiah said, "Lord, who has believed our report? "So, then faith comes by hearing, and hearing by the word of God.
> Romans 10:14-17

All three fronts must be faced with purity, holiness, truth, and steadfastness or no soul will ever be saved. Any person evangelizing who is not totally dedicated to Christ and living accordingly, will absolutely devastate the work of Christ, and will make the cross of Christ of noneffect. Ninety percent of what a person recognizes as truth is not from one's words but from his lifestyle, for as the apostle Paul wrote, "You are our epistle written in our hearts, known, and read by all men" (2 Corinthians 3:2).

The world knows how British journalist Henry Stanley went to Africa to find the famed missionary, Dr. David Livingstone. Stanley's greeting is world famous, "Dr. Livingstone, I presume?"[33] But few know the rest of the story. After the two had been together for some time, Stanley saw what Livingstone endured and wrote,

> I went to Africa as prejudiced as the biggest atheist in London. But there came for me a long time for reflection. I saw this solitary old man there and asked myself, "How on earth does he stop here, is he cracked, or what? What is it that inspires him so?" For months after we met, I found myself wondering at the old man carrying out all that was said in the Bible "Leave all things and follow me." But little by little his sympathy for others became contagious; my sympathy was aroused; seeing his piety, his gentleness, his zeal, his earnestness, and how he went about his business, I was converted by him.[34]

Father, forgive us for our lack in attitude toward evangelists and evangelism. Change our hearts. Start creating in us a laborer's heart and send us forth as laborers into the harvest. Help us to come to a full understanding of what you meant when you said, "The harvest truly is plentiful, but the laborers are few" (Matthew 9:37). Father, if you see a reason we are not called to go forth, give us a heart to actively support in every way possible those who are. Amen!

Remember, "A war not fought, is a war that can never be won." Can we truly allow Satan to fight a war for the souls of men with no opposition?

Chapter Questions To
Help Your Study

1. The Greek word for Evangelist means what?
2. Ephesians 4:11 leads us to think that Evangelists stand between apostles/prophets and pastors/teachers. True or False
3. A true evangelist is not a person who goes from church to church holding revivals. True or False
4. Everyone is commanded to Witness. True or False
5. Not everyone who witnesses is an Evangelist by calling. True or False
6. The Great commission has been given to the whole church. True or False
7. When was the last time you led someone to the Lord?
8. Perhaps the most significant factor that is generating the growth of the gospel around the world is
9. Winning souls is a war that is fought on three fronts. Name the three fronts.

PASTORS

And He Himself gave some to be apostles, some prophets, some evangelists, and some pastors and teachers.

Ephesians 4:11

Let us now look at the office of a Pastor. This office over many years of church history has been run down, despised, overlooked, traditionalized, glorified, idolized, and even cherished, but always misunderstood. With God's help, we will examine it and attempt to place it in its proper place of importance and honor.

The office of a pastor is just one of the five Administrative Gifts. It is not mentioned above or below any other, but in conjunction with the others. All the Administrative Gifts are intended to work in unison. This operational unity of the Gifts is very important. When these Gifts are properly used, they have specific beneficial purposes (Ephesians 4:12-16). Once again, they are:

1. for the equipping of the saint.
2. for the edifying of the body of Christ.
3. for unity of the faith.
4. for the knowledge of the Son of God.
5. for us to become a perfect man.
6. for the fullness of Christ.
7. that we should no longer be children, tossed to and fro.

8. so we are not carried about with every wind of doctrine.
9. so that we can speak the truth in love.
10. so that we may grow up in all things into Him who is the head—Christ.
11. for the effective working by which every part does its share.
12. to causes growth of the body.
13. for the edifying of itself in love.

God did not say any one office or combination of a few offices, would accomplish all this. These five offices must all work together in unison in order to achieve the best God has intended for His Body.

Many Bible scholars have improperly incorporated the apostolic, prophetic, evangelistic, and teaching aspects of the ministry into the job description of a pastor. While this is partially true, that a pastor must have ability to do them all, it is not true that a pastor is called to do them all. That is where the error lies. Because of this misunderstanding, many pastors try to be all things for their people; the result is that they usually fail, get burned out, and move on. This overloading of responsibly also greatly dilutes their effectiveness. This ineffectiveness results in the church being improperly equipped with the power and direction needed for the work God intended. This responsibility overload can also be attributed to the laity not stepping up into the calling God has placed upon them. It can also be due to the Pastor's inability to release control of any part of the ministry due to pride, arrogance, mistrust, lack of scriptural knowledge, insight, or in many cases a combination of all these factors. These pastors sincerely believe they are doing what is best for their flock, but they are sincerely mistaken. They are in fact doing the opposite by not allowing the implementation and operation of the proper apostolic order found in Ephesians 4:11. This is the main reason for the failure of many modernday churches to exhibit the omnipotent power and presence of God.

Another reason for the Church's ineffectiveness is that the office of a pastor is not one born out of the natural extension of the will, intellect, abilities, qualifications, or principles of man. Nor is the position of a pastor or any position for that matter one can train himself for, with the intent of one day becoming. No position is earned; it is a gift (And He Himself gave, Ephesians 4:11). You do not train yourself to become a pastor unless you already know you are called to be a pastor. Otherwise, the results will be ineffective at best.

Proper Christian training comes by doing two things. First: Rightly dividing the Word of God, so that if God does call someone to ministry, in whatever position He might choose, he will then be empowered to be a workman of God (2ⁿTimothy 2:15). Second: Work hard at knowing God intimately and constantly work at aligning one's lifestyle in accordance with His Word. Let us look at 2 Corinthians 3:2 again. This will help us to recognize and obey His calling. No matter one's qualifications or how much he studies, work, and desires to obtain a position; it will not be blessed by God unless God appoints him. It is only the Christian that knows God intimately and has the appropriate lifestyle who will be absolutely certain that God has called him to a specific ministry. It is only once a minister places himself in the center of God's will that his calling may truly be blessed by God.

Non-compliance with these simple God ordained protocols has caused scriptural obscureness, inconsistency, lack of power, direction, and scriptural error to infiltrate the Church. Many churches have not chosen those whom God has called and appointed. They have relied upon a candidate's earthly qualifications, training, looks, style, or charisma. The only way to receive all the benefits of God's plan for the Church is to go back and properly establish the divine apostolic order which is based on men God has chosen, and not on man's fleshly perception (1 Samuel 16:7).

It is fully understood that major problems like, loss of funds, people, confusion, and even the collapse of some ministries may occur as a result of such restorative actions. However, this would only be a short-term occurrence. In the long run, ministries would be healthier, larger, and more powerful, with more people saved and transformed into the image of God. The Church would have more power than can be imagined. The world and the body of Christ would be better for it. The most important benefit of this action is that we would once again be totally in line with God's ordained plan. God would then fill our houses of worship like never before.

In 1995, God called me to pastor a church in the Bronx. This calling came as a total shock because to this point in ministry, teaching was my only calling. In compliance with God's instruction, an application was presented and all tests and criteria required were met. To my surprise, the congregation chose another brother. After months of prayerful reflection on whether it was my own misunderstanding or if the word. I received was truly from God or if the church erred in their choice of candidates, I received a phone call from the head of the selection committee of that church. He called to apologize. He said that the entire board knew that I was called to that position but because this other brother had a more liberal view of Scripture and had a more outgoing personality, they felt that he was better suited for church growth, and, therefore, they decided to choose him. Six months after that the church was down to less than a dozen people and the pastor decided to walk off with no explanations. They called once again to inform me of the situation and ask if I would consider taking over the church. After several weeks of prayerful inquiries, God's answer came; my time had passed. I was to go to Israel, and upon my return, I was to teach at a Bible college. The church suffered six months of further hardship before God placed the right leadership in the church and started to restore the work there. The church has been doing wonderfully ever since.

One reason for a church choosing the wrong man to be their pastor and the resulting ineffectiveness of the church is the improper interpretation of the Scriptures. Many wellmeaning Bible studies have wrongly used the listed qualifications in 1 Timothy 3:2-7, Titus 1:5-9 and 1 Peter 5:1-5 to define the position of a "Pastor." Their argument is that the meaning of "episkopay" found in 1 Timothy 3:1 defines the work of an 'overseeing ministry," not the "office" of an overseer, and in their view, the Pastor is the overseeing ministry.

Although it is true that these passages list requirements needed to obtain a position of leadership in the church, there are several problems with using these scriptures to describe specifically the position of a pastor.

1. These requirements come under 'the category of works, not gifts. There are many true men of God that fulfill all of these qualifications and have the desire to become a pastor or an overseer, but do not have God's calling for the position. A pastor, like the other four administrative positions are Gifts. They cannot be earned! These Administrative Gifts can only be given by God, to the people whom God wills.

2. If you look closely at 1 Timothy 3:1 it specifically states what position is being described. It is not one of a Pastor but an Overseer or Bishop. Look carefully at what 1Timothy 3:1 says. "This is a faithful saying: If a man desires the office of a Bishop [overseer], he desires a good work",

3. The Greek word "episkopay" simply means to instigate, inspect, or to visit, one with oversight, a superintendent or one in charge. It is a noun in the Greek and it is presented in the feminine voice, making the word generic, or meaning the "office" of a Bishop, which it is so translated in the ASV, ESV, KJV, and the RSV just to name a few. This Greek word is used only four times in the New Testament. It is translated in Luke 19:44 and I Peter 2:12 as visitation, in Acts 1:20 as "bishoprick" (KJV) which means office, and in 1 Timothy 3:1 as an office of a Bishop. Some other translations say office of an Overseer. It does not mean nor is it ever translated pastor. Pastor is the Greek word "poimen," more on that in a moment.

Now look at 1 Timothy 3:2. The word, Bishop appears once again. This word in the Greek is "episkopos." "Episkopos" is the masculine form of the word found in verse one, which makes this word a specific person with the office of a Bishop. This form of the word for Bishop is used only five times in the New Testament (Acts 20:28, Philippians:1:1; 1 Timothy 3:2, Titus 1:7, and 1 Peter 2:25). In all cases, the word is translated either a specific bishop or bishops, or an overseer, depending on what translation is used, but never is it translated as the office of a Bishop.

This is extremely important to understand because neither Greek word Episkopay or Episkopos, is ever translated pastor, feeder, or shepherd anywhere in scripture. The Hebrew word for Pastor is roeh, which is translated shepherd. The rendering of the word roeh, or pastor is confined in the Old Testament to the book of Jeremiah (2:8, 3:15, 10:21, 12:10, 17:16, 22:22,23:1-2). And as stated earlier, the New Testament Greek word is "poimen" which is the Greek word used in Ephesians 4:11. "Poimen" means shepherd, or one who feeds. The word poimen appears seventeen times in the New Testament. While in Ephesians 4:11 it is rendered pastors, every other rendering is shepherd. Ephesians is also the only place where the word "poimen" is used where it does not refer directly to the Lord Jesus Christ, making Christ the most accurate example of a true pastor found anywhere in Scripture. Every other rendering of shepherd refers directly to Jesus Himself.

Nowhere in the Bible is a description of the specific duties of a Pastor found, yet, today almost the entire ministry of the church revolves around this one office. How did a ministry that is mentioned only once in the New Testament and not described anywhere come to dominate the life of the Body of Christ as it has? We are not implying that a pastor is less important than any other God ordained position, but the overwhelming desire to become a pastor over all other ministries has. The fact that a subject is not given much attention in Scripture does not necessarily reflect its level of importance either. For example, the Lord's Supper is only mentioned three times in scripture (Luke 22:19, 1 Corinthians 10: 16; 11:25). Being born again is only mentioned once and never defined, but is there anyone who would dispute its significance (John 3:7)?

The pastoral ministry is actually much more, not less, than what we now experience. it is also in many ways very different. Today the pastoral ministry has usurped much of the responsibility delegated to the other equipping ministries listed in Ephesians for the most part, pastors now have complete and total operational and directional authority in the church, while at the same time there is no unity or cooperation with the other Administrative Gifts.

On the other hand, many pastors have had much of their responsibility usurped. This usurping has come mostly by the spirit of the world, or "secular humanism." The pastoral ministry has been molded by man's desire to reach as many people as they can, anyway they can. The larger the numbers the better it is for the business of church, and the prestige that goes along with a large ministry. This is not true in every case mind you, but anyone who has been a Christian for any length of time knows this to be true. The pastoral ministry has also been usurped by board members who elect a new pastor based often times on their own agendas or how a prospective pastor looks or speaks and even the message he brings forth. If we want to see the Church of Christ once again operating in the fullness of glory and power, and doing the work it was designed for, it is imperative that we design our churches according to the Lord's complete operational method, which is outlined in Ephesians 4:11. We must choose our pastors by knowing the heart of God. Knowing the heart of God only comes through much prayer and fasting.

All ministries are the manifestation of an aspect of the Lord's own ministry. The position of a Pastor is one of those aspects. Therefore, by observing the ministry of Jesus who is our Great Shepherd, we can recognize that calling in others and ourselves. Jesus was God's apostle, prophet, evangelist, pastor or shepherd, and teacher. A minister in one of those positions should become an empty and willing vessel, through which the Lord reveals Himself in order to touch the needs of His people. The Lord never did anything or went anywhere the Father did not order him to go. God's chosen ministers should act in exactly the same manner.

Our Spiritual authority comes by knowing our calling and its limitations. We must remain in the authority and position appointed to us. This is why the apostle Paul explained that he was careful not to go beyond the sphere of apostolic authority that God had appointed to him (2 Corinthians 10:13-14). Many ministries are suffering because they have obscured their positional boundaries. The Church is full of God called ministers who are limited in power and scope. This limitation comes because they have entered geographical areas without an appointment, or they have taken on spiritual jobs for which they are not called. When we stay within the realm that the Lord has appointed, the work becomes easy because He is colaboring with us. When we go beyond our calling however, the job becomes burdensome and saps us of our strength, and our anointing. If we discover the proper boundaries and responsibilities of our calling, and stay within them, the result will be an increase in our anointing and effectiveness.

What exactly is a Pastor? What exactly does the pastoral ministry entail? Paul's Pastoral Epistles, which are first and second Timothy and Titus, contain the sum and substance of New Testament teaching on the subject. In these books, Paul lays out three general functions we can look to for information and instruction on what a pastoral ministry should be.

1. Pastors are to administrate worship services. This administration includes the order of worship, administering the sacraments, and preaching the Word. In this capacity, the Pastor is appropriately termed a "minister" (2 Timothy 4:2-5).

2. A Pastor's responsibilities spring out of the former. They include the feeding of the flock, the instruction of its

members in all aspects of life, and bringing every soul to Christian maturity. Pastors or "under shepherds" must imitate the chief shepherd, who "calls His sheep by name" (Titus 2).

3. The pastoral relation with his flock passes naturally into what we have scriptural authority for calling, "the spiritual government of the Church." Its ministers are called rulers, and all its members are bidden to obey them that have rule (1 Timothy 6:1-2; Titus 3:1).

4. Pastors are also commanded to be watchful (Hebrews 13:17; 1 Timothy 4:5). They must be on guard for any predator that might try to destroy the work of God in the flock.

5. They are to be gentle and affectionate (1 Thessalonians 2:7-8) treating every problem, whether large or small with the same decorum.

6. Pastors are also instructed to exhort, warn, and com fort their flock (1 Thessalonians 2:11; 1 Corinthians 4:14-15).

The Pastor's spiritual authority includes the physical, emotional, mental, and spiritual aspects of his flock's lives. But he is not a sovereign ruler who cannot be questioned. The ultimate and final authority lies with God and His Word. That is why you are commanded to "be diligent to present yourself approved to God, a worker who does not need to be ashamed, rightly dividing the word of truth" (2 Timothy 2:15). So, when the man of God who is both finite and fallible is in error or goes astray, we will be aware of it. That is why the Word of God also says, "By the mouth of two or three witnesses every word shall be established" (2 Corinthians 13:1). On the other hand, if a man of God comes in his proper authority and makes a ruling that is based upon the Word of God, we must be obedient, even though that ruling conflicts with or impacts our life style.

The Greek word "poimen" is also translated feeder. This translation reveals the basic function of the pastoral ministry. It is to feed the Lord's sheep so that the Lord's sheep can grow into the fullness of Christ. We may think that feeding the flock really means the pastor must also be a teacher, which is listed after the Pastor in Ephesians 4:11. However, the word teacher is a different Greek word than that of Pastor.

The Greek word for teacher in Ephesians 4:11, is "didaskalos," and it is more accurately translated instructor. And even though there can be a combination of these Gifts in any of the administrative offices, there are also many who are called and gifted to teach who have little pastoral ability, and many gifted with pastoral abilities who have little teaching ability. Therefore, there is little problem seeing them as distinct from each other.

What is the difference then between feeding and instructing? Feeding has to do with providing the complete diet, while instructing has more to do with developing skills. At a university, for example, the chef would do the feeding, and the professors do the instructing. How much would a student learn and how healthy would he be if our churches did the same, and not allow professors to feed and chefs to train. Would we not have a much higher quality of spiritual food to serve and better instruction in every aspect of God's Word and work, resulting in a betterquality disciple? Wouldn't a concentration on only one aspect of the ministry leave the pastor more time to spend in the presence of the Master? Wouldn't he then be better able to properly feed his sheep? Would you agree that the feeding of the Lord's sheep is critical and should be given the highest priority? It would be unthinkable to give the King of King's own household poorly prepared, half done or junk food.

In biblical times, as we can see in the story of Joseph in the pharaoh's prison, the baker was one of the king's most trusted servants. The baker was considered a most honored position. What chef then, who was given the commission to prepare the meals for the president, or any potentate, would not put his very best into each meal? Such a chef would probably scour the world for the best ingredients. He would hire only the best assistants.

He would seek out only the best dinnerware on which to serve the meal. How much more should we put our best into what we serve the Lord or His bride? Serving the Lord's bride is an incredible honor. Shouldn't a pastor or any minister prepare every message they serve with more devotion than the greatest chef would? This type of dedication takes many hours and tremendous work and diligence. It leaves little time for all the other ministries, with which pastors burden themselves.

Moses had this same problem, didn't he? What was Jethro's advice to Moses? Moses recognized his father in law's advice as godly for he immediately obeyed that Word of the Lord. Shouldn't all of us in every aspect of our lives consider obeying that advice (Exodus 18:13-24)?

What about the story in Acts 6? Did not the apostles tell the church to choose seven men of good reputation to serve God's people, men who were full of the Holy Spirit and wisdom? What was the apostle's reason for that decision? They said, "It is not reason that we [the apostles] should leave the Word of God, and serve tables...But we will give ourselves continually to prayer and to the ministry of the Word" (Acts 6:2, 4 KJV). Didn't that please the multitude (verse 5)? Again, shouldn't we do the same?

In Matthew 24:45-46, which is the Lord's discourse concerning the last days, Jesus includes a challenging statement that is obviously directed at the pastoral ministry. "Who then is a faithful and wise servant, whom his master made ruler over his household to give them food in due season? Blessed is that servant whom his master, when he comes, will find so doing" (Emphasis added). Here we see that the ones whom the Lord calls to feed His sheep are "put in charge of His household," because of the important need for His people having the proper spiritual food, the Lord has made a "faithful and wise servant" the ruler of His house. When was the last time you saw a manager of a company do everything? Never! He hires help to do the work. He oversees and directs the business in a way that is in accordance with the wishes of the owner.

Also, we see in Matthew 24:45-46 how critically important it is to feed the flock at the exact time necessary. The food should not only by pure, delicious and containing all the proper nutrients. It should also be given in due season. This insures a healthy body. The pastor is the manager over the Lord's household. He is chosen and called because he is a faithful and wise servant. Note also, although he has been given authority over the flock, he is still a servant not the potentate. It is his responsibility to make sure that the body he has been entrusted with is healthy and well fed. A "faithful and wise servant" is one who is found so doing (verse 46).

Before we close this chapter, let's look at one more section of scripture, John 21:15-17.

So, when they had 'eaten breakfast, Jesus said to Simon Peter, "Simon, son of Jonah, do you love Me more than these?" He said to Him, "Yes, Lord, you know that 1 love You." He said to him, "Feed My lambs." He said to him again a second time, "Simon, son of Jonah, do you love Me?" He said to Him, "Yes, Lord; You know that I love You." He said to him, "Tend My sheep." He said to him the third time, "Simon, son of Jonah, do you love Me?" Peter was grieved because He said to him the third time, "Do you love Me?" And he said to Him, "Lord, you know all things; You know that I love You." Jesus said to him, "Feed My sheep."

In this section of scripture, the Lord is giving three different instructions to Peter, first it was to feed the lambs, then to tend the sheep, and finally to feed the sheep.

Notice the Lord made a distinction between the two words feeding" and tending. Most of us would agree that they are different. Feeding means to make sure proper food is available for the sheep. Tending denotes a watching over, for protection, nursing, and discipline. All these are typical of the modern pastor's duties. It is also noteworthy that the Lord based Peter's responsibility to the sheep on Peter's love for Him. Not on Peter's love for the sheep.

Each command for Peter's love for the sheep came after the question, "Peter. Do you love me?" Understanding this makes it clear that the foundation of any ministry must be the person's love for the Lord, not the sheep. If we love the Lord more than His people, we will love His people unconditionally. If we love the people more than we love the Lord, our duty shifts from obeying God to obeying the people. The result will be that the will of the people will inevitably outweigh the will of God. In other words, we become idolaters! Jesus is then reduced from a navigator to a spectator.

In the pastoral ministry, many pastors will unavoidably be faced with problems that they do not know how to handle. This will also be true of any minister or Christian for that matter. Two things must happen: One: Pastors must ask God and keep asking Him until the answer arrives. They must seek to find the answer in God's Word, they must knock until the Lord opens the door and gives help. Two: They must seek counsel from other mature and wise brethren (Proverbs 24:6; 27:9).

Jesus met the needs of all who came to Him. He did it by loving the Father first and foremost. His ministry emanated from that relationship. All ministries must extend from the same relationship. If your relationship with the Father is strong, your ministry will be strong. If your relationship with the Father is weak, your ministry will be weak. The key to fulfilling one's ministry is to love the Lord unconditionally, obey His commands, and earnestly seek to be changed into the Master's image.

Our goal is clear, and it is quite a journey back to the basic truths of Jesus' instructions. Every journey no matter how long and hard, starts with the first step. Pastors must undertake that journey. Pastors are not called to be all, and do all. They are faithful and wise servants that must supervise the feeding and tending of the sheep God gave them. Pastors must spend their time with the Lord in prayer and Bible study. They are not to do every menial task set before them. Pastors must take the Lord's yoke, not the ministry's yoke. The Lord's yoke is easy to bear. The ministry's yoke will become unbearable and will eventually break them under its weight. Good shepherds must learn to align the Lord's ministry after the pattern set down by Christ. We must look for and petition the Lord for all the administrative offices to come alive in the Body of Christ. Then once they are discovered, we must use them. We must not hold them back, but have faith in those whom God has chosen.

As parishioners, we must discover our calling and fulfill it. We must hold up our pastor's arms in prayer and in action. We must do unto him as we would have him do unto us. We must learn to give more than receive. We must seek rather to comfort then to be comforted, to understand rather than to be understood. We must bear his burdens, not be his burden.

Chapter Questions To
Help Your Study

1. The Hebrew and Greek word used for "Pastor" is translated
2. The most accurate example of a true pastor is found in whom?
3. Paul lays out three general functions we can look to for instruction regarding the Pastoral Ministry. What are they?
4. Pastors are also commanded to be what?
5. The Pastor's spiritual authority falls into every area of his flock's life. True or False
6. In John 21:15-17, the Lord made a distinction between what? What does this tell you?

TEACHERS

And He Himself gave some to be apostles, some prophets, some evangelists, and some pastors and teachers.

Ephesians 4:11

Notice the way teachers is inserted into this verse. It is the only Administrative Gift that is not preceded by the word some. Notice that the conjunctive word "and" is inserted instead. The use of this conjunction, and the omission of the article "some" from before the word teachers causes a number of my esteemed brethren to think that these two offices are in fact part of the same office. This implies that the duties of feeding and teaching are assigned to the office of Pastor. However, while it is true that no man is fit to be a pastor who cannot teach and a teacher needing the knowledge which pastoral experience gives does not mean that the two offices are one and the same. The combining of varied experiences is helpful in all the Administrative Gifts.

The word Pastor, as we discussed in the last chapter, is the New Testament Greek word "poimen." Only in Ephesians 4:11 is "poimen" translated pastors. Every other rendering in the New Testament is shepherd. The Greek word translated pastor or shepherd, can also be translated feeder. This translation reveals the basic function of this ministry. The New Testament Greek word for teacher is not "poimen;" it is "didaskalos". "Didaskalos" means instructor. The difference then between a pastor/feeder and a teacher/instructor is that feeding has to do with providing a spiritual diet, while instructing has to do with developing skills.

You may think, the function of a Pastor must include teaching, and you would be right. That doesn't make the office one of a pastor/teacher. Look at it like this. When a child is born, the parents feed the child, change the child, and protect the child. As the child grows, the parents tell the child what is right and wrong, good and evil, proper and improper, moral and immoral. Doing these things does not help the child mature grow and intellectually advance unless they can also properly instruct the child by answering the questions of why and how. That is the job of a teacher.

A teacher is empowered by God to answer the questions why and how. Why is it moral? Why is it wrong? Why is it evil? How do I avoid evil? Not just that it is, moral or wrong, but why it is moral or wrong, and how do I avoid what is wrong, how do I avoid evil, and how do I act morally? This is not to mention learning such basic skills as reading, writing, arithmetic, science etc. Moreover, added to this comes the how. How do we accomplish or complete the task God sets before us? As you can see, this is the job of a teacher. In this illustration, I am not implying that one office is more important than the other or the two offices cannot be accomplished by one person. This illustration only shows the difference between the two offices.

Here is another illustration. Our youngest son, Aaron, came home last year with a problem in math. The problem included time and speed. Which train would arrive first in Los Angeles? Train A, traveling at 160 miles per hour nonstop from New York to Los Angeles, a total of 3200 miles, or Train B, traveling at 90 miles per hour nonstop from Saint Louis to Los Angeles, a distance of 2100 miles. Now most of us without thinking too hard would say Train A, and we would be right. However, what Aaron needed was the mathematical formula used to figure out the correct answer. Here lies instruction. Telling Aaron that Train A will arrive first, will not help him get the answer the next time a similar question is asked, but teaching Aaron mathematically why and how we arrived at that answer will!

There are many times when a hurting individual just needs to be shown that he is loved, or when only comfort, a kind word, an attentive ear, or a loving touch will satisfy his need. There will also be times when saving that person's life is the most important thing. For example, a person who is about to fall off a cliff does not need to be told what gravity is, how gravity works, and what will happen when that person releases his grip and hits the ground. Doing that would be absolutely ludicrous. What that person desperately needs, more than anything else, is a strong solidly grounded compassionate person to secure him. That is why God gave pastors. There are many other times however, that a person heading for a cliff does not need to be comforted or walked with; he needs to be instructed in the right direction to walk in order to avoid the cliff. That is the job of the teacher.

As stated earlier, the Greek word for teacher in the New Testament is "didaskalos." It is important to note that variations of the word "didaskalos, nomodidaskalos, and kalodidaskalos" carry the meaning of a teacher of right, truth, and good things. It also means a teacher, one who expounds the law; who is a doctor of truth. As we all know, the Gospel of Jesus is good news. It is truth! There is also another word in the New Testament that carries the same meaning as "didaskalos, nomodidaskalos, and kalodidaskalos" and that word is "euaggelizo." "Euaggelizo" is a word related to "euaggelistes," which is the Greek word for evangelist and is translated to preach, declare, or to bring forth glad tidings, especially the Gospel. What these Greek words show us is that a teacher's divine duty is to instruct God's children in what is right, pure, and undefiled. God's Word tells us that people are delivered from the bondage of sin and built up in righteousness through the agency of the truth. God's Word is the truth (John 17:17). That makes teaching imperative.

What is the definition of Teaching in a Biblical sense? What are the general and specific aims of a Bible Teacher? The definition of Bible teaching is the communication of the Gospel (Good News) through formal and informal educational programs so that the facts of Scripture can be presented clearly and completely. This allows individuals the ability to respond by personal faith in Christ so that they can grow toward spiritual maturity. The teacher's ministry is an equipping ministry to all age levels that nurtures spiritual growth and evangelistic outreach. Its general aim is to transmit the Word of God so that every student may be transformed into God's image. "For the word of God is living and powerful, and sharper than any two edged sword, piercing even to the division of soul and spirit, and of joints and marrow, and is a discerner of the thoughts and intents of the heart" (Hebrews 4:12).

Teachers must recognize and accept their responsibility to lead each student to trust in Christ and accept Him as their personal Savior. Acceptance of Christ as Savior is only the first step toward a full life; however, you should not be satisfied to stop there. It is God's purpose that every Christian "grow in the grace and knowledge of our Lord and Savior Jesus Christ" (2 Peter 3:18). And "be conformed into the image of his Son, that he might be the firstborn among many brethren" (Romans 8:29).

It is also important to note that teaching is a command from Jesus Himself. It is a New Testament pattern we are to follow. In Matthew 28:19-20 Jesus tells us to "go therefore and make disciples of all the nations, baptizing them in the name of the Father and of the Son and of the Holy Spirit, "teaching them to observe all things that I have commanded you; and lo, I am with you always, even to the end of the age." Amen. Acts 5:42 gives us the New Testament pattern. "And daily in the temple, and in every house, they did not cease teaching [didasko to teach] and preaching "euaggelizo" [to announce good news] Jesus as the Christ." Please notice they are not the same. One is specifically for learning the other is declaring that Jesus is the Christ. Why? Because teaching enables many new lives to come to Christ for salvation and grow in grace and be transformed into His image. This can only come through learning His precepts. The patient and dedicated teaching of God's Word is essential in meeting this end. It is, therefore, a teacher's responsibility to link the truths taught with the daily lives of the students in order to help them become "doers of the word, and not hearers only, deceiving yourselves" (James 1:22). Only believers who possess and profess the truth will be thus transformed.

Teaching is also the primary root of the commission that Christ gave to His apostles before His ascension. "Go," said He, "teach all nations." In this way, we will make disciples. A disciple is one who is "taught" to obey the principles of his master. The term disciple is principally used of the followers of Christ. How can a person go and make disciples if there are no teachers to teach them? Being taught is one of the precious promises of God's covenant with man. All Children of God shall be "taught of the Lord and great shall be the peace of thy Children" (Isaiah 54:13). Jesus quoted this verse in Isaiah and He adds a promise to it. "Therefore, everyone who has heard and learned from the Father comes to Me" (John 6:45). Not only will great peace be the children's inheritance, but also, they are given an open invitation to come into the Father's presence at any time. What an awesome responsibility for the teacher? What a tremendous promise to those who would be taught? These promises are not given to any of the other administrative ministries. Only to those who teach. That is why if anyone undertakes, teaching in Christian assemblies, he shall receive a stricter judgment. "My brethren, let not many of you become teachers, knowing that you will receive a stricter judgment" (James 3:1).

Notice that it is the Teachers that are the ones who are held in stricter judgment. This admonition is not given to Pastors, Evangelists or any of the other Administrative Gifts, just Teachers. There is however, a terrible end, pronounced upon any minister of the Gospel that would proclaim a false Gospel.

> I marvel that you are turning away so soon from Him who called you in the grace of Christ, to a different gospel, which is not another, but there are some who trouble you and want to pervert the Gospel of Christ. But even if we, or an angel from

heaven, preach [Euaggelizo] any other gospel to you than what we have preached to you, let him be accursed As we have said before, so now I say again, if anyone preaches any other gospel to you than what you have received, let him be accursed.

Galatians 1:6-9

Accursed is the Greek word "anathema." Meaning, one which, in God's righteous judgment, is pronounced doomed to destruction, because they will lead the children of God away from the atoning work accomplished by the death of Christ. The real possibility of being led astray from the true Gospel by false leaders was brought to fruition in the Galatian church. That is the reason why as God's children you are strictly commanded to "be diligent to present yourself approved to God, a worker who does not need to be ashamed, rightly dividing the word of truth" (2 Timothy 2:15). God's children must be prepared to recognize lies so: "that we should no longer be children, tossed to and fro and carried about with every wind of doctrine, by the trickery of men, in the cunning craftiness of deceitful plotting" (Ephesians 4:14)

False teachers have but one desire and that is to exploit you. Look at the warning Peter gives.

But there were also false prophets among the people, even as there will be false teachers among you, who will secretly bring in destructive heresies, even denying the Lord who bought them, and bring on themselves swift destruction. And many will follow their destructive ways, because of whom the way of truth will be blasphemed. By covetousness they will exploit you with deceptive words; for a long time, their judgment has not been idle, and their destruction does not slumber.

2 Peter 2:13

Teaching, as discussed earlier, is an essential root of the commission that Christ gave His disciples before His ascension. These God appointed men and women have a tremendous calling and an awesome responsibility to teach accurately and faithfully the Word of God. We have also seen that they will fall under stricter judgment if they do not.

Teachers, based on the reasons given above, have three specific proposes when they are teaching.

1. Increasing knowledge. "The entrance of Your words gives light; It gives understanding to the simple."

   Psalm 119:130

   This Book of the Law shall not depart from your mouth, but you shall meditate in it day and night, that you may observe to do according to all that is written in it. For then you will make your way prosperous, and then you will have good success.

   Joshua 1:8

2. Changing attitudes. "For I say to you, that unless your righteousness exceeds the righteousness of the scribes and Pharisees, you will by no means enter the kingdom of heaven."

   Matthew 5:20

3. Improving behavior. "But He said, more than that, blessed are those who hear the word of God and keep it!" Notice also what James 2:26 says; "For as the body without the spirit is dead, so faith without works is dead also."

   Luke 11:28

The fact is that three out of four Christians became Christians during the teen years. Teaching, especially to young adults during these learning years is crucial to the well being of their Christian life.

Jesus said in Matthew 9:37-38, "Then He said to His disciples, the harvest truly is plentiful, but the laborers are few. 'Therefore, pray the lord of the harvest to send out laborers into His harvest.' We see that there are two things this verse stresses. First, is to save, and second is to send out. We must give all men the knowledge that will lead them to Christ and then prepare them with the knowledge and desire to reap an already prepared harvest. These two principles explain why the Great Commission to teach is so great and the punishment so severe.

Finally, let us look at the benefits that will be received by learning the Word of God taught by truthful and anointed teachers, who have done accurate and diligent study. In 2 Timothy 3:16-17, Paul says, "All Scripture is given by inspiration of God, and is profitable for doctrine, for reproof, for correction, for instruction in righteousness, that the man of God may be complete, thoroughly equipped for every good work."

A. It is profitable for Doctrine.	Doctrines are rules to live by
B. It is profitable for Reproof.	Reproof is conviction or evidence needed to convince one, of the errors of his ways. 1 Corinthians 10:11 says, "Now all these things happened to them as examples, and they were written for our admonition, upon whom the ends of the ages have come."
C. It is profitable for Correction.	Correction means to rectify one's errors to make one worthy again.

D. It is profitable for Instruction.	Instruction means to be directed, and guided along the straight and narrow path that leads to the Promised Land. In Acts 18:26 Paul speaking about Apollos says, "he began to speak boldly in the synagogue. When Aquila and Priscilla heard him, they took him aside and explained to him the way of God more accurately."
E. It is profitable for Righteousness.	Righteousness means to be made equitable, or right or just with God. "My tongue shall speak of your word, for all your commandments are righteousness (Psalm 119 :172).
F. It will make us Complete.	Complete means to be at a place of being mature, accomplished, and totally furnished having all the tools necessary to be a true man or women of God

Let's look at other Scriptures that will bring to light other benefits of learning God's Word.

G. It will cleanse our way.	In Psalms 119:9 the psalmist says, "How can a young man cleanse his way? By taking heed according to Your word." And in John 15:3 Jesus says, "You are already clean because of the word which I have spoken to you."
H. It gives light and understanding	In Psalm 119:130 the psalmist says, "The entrance of Your words gives light; It gives understanding to the simple."
I. It is profitable for Sanctification.	In John 17:17 Jesus says, "Sanctify them by Your truth. Your word is truth."

J. It is profitable for Faith.

In John 20:31 Jesus says, "but these are written that you may believe that Jesus is the Christ, the Son of God, that believing you may have life in His name."

K. It is profitable for Hope

in Romans 15:4 Paul says, "For whatever things were written before were written for our learning, that we through the patience and comfort of the Scriptures might have hope."

L. It will purify your Soul.

In I Peter 1:22 Peter says, "Since you have purified your souls in obeying the truth through the Spirit in sincere love of the brethren, love one another fervently with a pure heart,"

M. It gives assurance of Salvation

In 1 John 5:13 John says, "These things I have written to you who believe in the name of the Son of God, that you may know that you have eternal life, and that you may continue to believe in the name of the Son of God."

N. It will make you Wise.

In 2 Timothy 3:15 Paul says to Timothy, "and that from childhood you have known the Holy Scriptures, which are able to make you wise for salvation through faith which is in Christ Jesus."

The office of a teacher must be fully restored and operating at full strength in the Body of Christ if we are ever to see the coming of the Lord Jesus Christ. With this restoration, the Body of Christ will get stronger. She will start to take her rightful place in the kingdom. Many strongholds of the enemy will be torn down. Many souls will be saved and firmly planted. Many false doctrines will be revealed and the false teachers, who are spreading them, will be uncovered and removed.

There is a long way to go before we get there and it is only the divine reestablishing of all the Administrative Gifts in their proper order and function that will get us there. Remember the Lord Jesus Christ is going to return, and catch His bride away. "That He might present her to Himself a glorious church, not having spot or wrinkle or any such thing, but that she should be holy and without blemish" (Ephesians 5:27). "Therefore, beloved, looking forward to these things, be diligent to be found by Him in peace, without spot and blameless" (2 Peter 3:14).

The only way to achieve the maturing of the saints, so that all of us may grow into His fullness, is through the operational unity of the five Administrative Gifts. Each one must work in unison with each other and in each congregation (Refer again to Ephesians 4:12-16). Not the least of these is God anointed, God appointed, and God ordained teachers.

Let us all take time each day to pray and ask God to complete the work of restoring all His Administrative Gifts to full unity of operation. Let us also pray that God will bestow upon His bride all the benefits of that operation as well. This will shorten the time remaining before the glorious appearing of our Lord and Savior Jesus Christ.

Chapter Questions To
Help Your Study

1. The word "teacher" is a different Greek word, which could be more accurately translated "Instructor" True or False
2. So what is the difference then between "feeding" and "instructing?"
3. It's a teacher's divine duty to teach that which is right, pure, and undefiled. True or False
4. Teaching is an essential root of the commission that Christ gave to His apostles before His ascension. True or False
5. The benefits of learning the Word of God either by accurate and diligent study or truthful and anointed teaching is?

HELPS AND ADMINISTRATIONS

We will continue our study of the Spiritual. Gifts with a look at the Gift of Helps and Administrations/ Governments. These Gifts, though not mentioned in Ephesians 4:11 are as vital to the operation of the Church as those Gifts already discussed. The Gifts of Helps and Administrations are listed in 1 Corinthians 12:28. "And God has appointed these in the church: first apostles, second prophets, third teachers, after that miracles, then gifts of healings, helps, administrations, varieties of tongues).

Helps is translated from the Greek word 'Antilepsis." properly signifies a laying hold of, an exchange (anti) to take as in support. It means to take a burden upon oneself instead of another, in order to give an individual relief or freedom to pursue other matters. Though there is no definition given in Scripture regarding these Gifts, there are clues that give us insight into its function in the Body of Christ. Here are some. Acts 6:1-6 refers to the ministry of helps as to helping the weak and needy so the disciples could devote their time to prayer and the study of the Word. Numbers 11:17 refers to the ministry of helps by way of helping with one's time and means. One commentator defines the injunction "support the weak" found in 1 Thessalonians 5:14, as those who, like the household of Stephanas (1 Corinthians 16:15), devote themselves to ministering to the saints. Hort defines the ministration as "anything that would be done for the poor, weak, or outcast brethren."[35] Unger defines it as "the ministrations of the deacons, who have care of the sick as in 1 Corinthians 12:28 where it is used in the sense of helpers."[36] Strong defines it "as one who gives relief to another."[37]

It is important to note that all these educated brothers refer to the Gift of Helps as:

1. A Gift of God given to the Body of Christ.
2. An office with special recognition.
3. Calling this office and the gifted individuals Deacons or Elders.
4. A Gift that will never be done away with, (1 Corinthians 13:8).

All of us at one time or another has seen a precious brother or sister come into our congregation, and with a humble and contrite heart do anything that is asked of them. They never question the validity of the request; they just go about doing whatever they are asked. They go on, repairing whatever they find broken or supporting whatever minister or ministry that needs supporting. They do these things without looking or asking for recognition. They do what must be done without taking any glory for themselves. They never get in the way of those who strive for that recognition. These men and women of God truly are some of the greatest in the Kingdom of God (Matthew 20:25-28). They should never be discouraged or downtrodden or questioned; they should only be guided, and encouraged! These blessed individuals are as important to the work of the ministry as the apostles, prophets, evangelists, pastors and teachers, because without them ministers cannot spend their valuable time doing what they should be doing, "giving ourselves continually to prayer and to the ministry of the word" (Acts 6:4).

The late Dr. Roy Gray, a Bible College professor at East Texas Bible College and Miracle Valley Bible College, once told us that He believed when the roll call in heaven is made to crown the greatest in the kingdom of God, it will not be the greatest Evangelist, nor will it be the greatest Pastor or Apostle. He believed that it would be one of these blessed helpers of whom nobody has ever heard. He believed all the spiritual weapons at our disposal, and all the power God has granted us, would be useless if we are preoccupied fighting earthly problems. These helpers give the time and support God's warriors need to fight the spiritual enemy, and to walk in their callings (Ref. Acts 6:1-7).

Now let us look at the Gift of Governments. The word "kubernesis" which is the Greek word used in 1 Corinthians 12:28 translated Governments in the Old King James Version, can also be correctly translated Administrations, and is translated as such in the New American Standard and New International Versions. The word simply means to guide or govern. These terms indicate steering or piloting. To better understand the meaning and operation of the office of Administrations/Governments, it would greatly benefit us to note other ways that the Greek word "kubernesis" is used. "Kubernesis" is used to mean a servant in Matthew 22:13, 23:11 and Mark 9:35. A minister in Matthew 20:26 Mark 10:43 and Romans 13:4, 15:8, and a deacon in Philippians 1:1 and in 1 Thessalonians 3:8, 12. These are the men and women of God that direct and govern the programs that feed the saints on a physical level. These individuals though often times called upon to set their hands to the plow and do the work themselves in no way changes the fact that their main calling is to administrate the physical duties needed by the ministry, the church, and the building, so the planting done by the other ministers will produce thirty, sixty and hundredfold fruit.

Fredrick Louis Godet in his commentary on 1 Corinthians tells us that "governments or administrations, no doubt denotes the various kinds of superintendence needed for the external good order of the assemblies and of the worship of the Church. For it was necessary to find and furnish the places of meeting, etc. This all requires what we should nowadays call committees, with their presidents."[38]

In addition, the Jamieson, Fausset and Brown commentary tells us that,

> These officers, though now ordinary and permanent, were originally specially endowed with the Spirit for their office. Government being occupied with externals, despite the outward status it gives, is ranked with the lower functions. "He that giveth" [answering to "Helps"} "he that rules" [answering to "governments"].[39] Matthew Henry's commentary states, that the difference between the Gift of Helps and the Gift of Governments or Administrations is; "Helps, or such as had the compassion on the sick and weak, and ministered to them; "Governments," or such as had the disposal of the charitable contributions of the church, and dealt them out to the poor.[40]

Another example of the difference of the Gift of Helps and Governments or Administrations is found in Romans 12:6-8.

> Having then gifts differing according to the grace that is given to us, let us use them: if prophecy, let us prophesy in proportion to our faith; or ministry, let us use it in our ministering; he who teaches, in teaching; he who exhorts, in exhortation; he who gives, with liberality; he who leads, with diligence; he who shows mercy, with cheerfulness.

Let's also look at 1 Timothy 3:8-12 for other qualifications these men and women of God who possess the Gift of Governments must have.

Likewise, deacons (kubernesis) must be reverent, not double-tongued, not given to much wine, not greedy for money, holding the mystery of the faith with a pure conscience. But let these also first be tested; then let them serve as deacons, being found blameless. Likewise, their wives must be reverent, not slanderers, temperate, faithful in all things. Let deacons be the husbands of one wife, ruling their children and their own houses well.

These men and women of God, who by calling, hold the office of governments,

1. are to be the servants of all (Matthew 20:2, 23:11)
2. are to execute wrath on evil (Romans 13:4).
3. are ministers of the New Covenant, in order to give life (2 Corinthians 3:5-9).
4. are to be ministers of Righteousness (2 Corinthians 3:5-9),
5. are to be ministers of Reconciliation (2 Corinthians 5:18);
6. must not give offense in anything; (2 Corinthians 6:3)
7. are to remain blameless (2 Corinthians 6:3).
8. are to be ministers of Christ (2 Corinthians 11:23)
9. are to be steadfast and grounded continuing in the faith, not moved from the hope of the Gospel (Colossians 1:23);
10. their stewardship is not given by man but is only given by God (Colossians 1:25).
11. are to be sanctified by the Word of God and prayer (1 Timothy 4:5).
12. are to be able to instruct others traveling the same way (1 Timothy 4:6, 11).
13. should not be belittled or looked upon as unimportant in any way. Instead, they are "due double honor, as due to all who labor in the word and doctrine" (1 Timothy 5:17).

Chapter Questions To
Help Your Study

1. The Greek word for Helps is "antilepsis." It properly signifies a laying hold of, an exchange (anti), to take or to lay hold of as in support. True or False
2. Great men of God refer to the Gift of Helps as what? Name the four things referred to.
3. The word "kubernesis" which is the Greek word used in 1 Corinthians 12:28 for Administrations is translated the word simply means to guide or govern, which denotes steering, or piloting. True or False

1ST CORINTHIANS 13 AND SPIRITUAL GIFTS

The main texts for our study on the Spiritual Gifts have been Ephesians 4 and 1Corinthians 12 & 14. However, sandwiched between 1 Corinthians 12 and 14 is, as many call it the Love Chapter. 1 Corinthians 13 is not an interlude between chapters 12 and 14 but an interlink between the two. The divine placement of this chapter shows that there is a definite correlation between the Spiritual Gifts and Love, and that they must have a working relationship. Therefore, it is vital that we turn our attention to 1st Corinthians 13 to see what that working relationship is.

Many believe that in 1st Corinthians 13 Paul was just defining another spiritual gift. If one looks at only the first two verses combined with Paul's climax to the chapter, one might be influenced to agree and come to the conclusion that love is not only a spiritual gift but also the greatest of all spiritual gifts.

Let us look at what 1 Corinthians 13:1-2, 13 says.

> Though I speak with the tongues of men and of angels, but have not love, I have become sounding brass or a clanging cymbal. and though I have the gift of "Prophecy and understand all mysteries and all knowledge, and though I have all faith, so that I could remove mountains, but have not love, I am nothing… And now abide faith, hope, love, these three; but the greatest of these is love.

There is no question on what God's love has inspired and imparted to this sin filled, wretched world. And there is no argument on what love has inspired and imparted is the greatest of all God's Gifts. However, when love is properly classified, it is not a Gift but a Fruit of the Spirit (Galatians 5:22). Love is God's very essence and nature. In 1 John 4:8 John says, "God is love!"

Let us now look at this marvelous and extraordinary Fruit of the Spirit, called Love (Agape in the Greek) and its relationship to the Gifts of the Spirit. Before we begin however, let's take another look at 1 Corinthians 13.

In the chapter on the Classification and Motivation of Spiritual Gifts, we stated that 1 Corinthians 13 is not a study on God's love, nor is it, an examination, and definition of Love as explained in the context of understanding God's love itself! And it does not define Love as a Spiritual Gift. The subject of 1 Corinthians 13 is: Love as the motivational power and purpose for having and using all Spiritual Gifts. 1 Corinthians 13 shows the relationship between Love and Spiritual Gifts, by comparing Spiritual Gifts without Love and Spiritual Gifts with Love!

Let me illustrate. Imagine you are in a car. You are driving to a place you have only heard about but to which you have never been. You are not sure of the direction, how far your destination is, or how hard a road you must travel. In this situation, two elements are vital to arriving at your desired destination safely. One is the fuel you will need to get there, and the other is a road map that will show you the right path. As Christians, we are driving the car; Christ's likeness is our destination. We do not know what direction to go, how long, or hard the journey might be. In the process of getting to our destination, we must avoid wrong turns, treacherous roads, roadblocks, and dead ends. In order to do this, we must have a good detailed road map that will show us the safest and most accurate way to travel.

Spiritual Gifts and Love are the two essential elements needed for the trip. Love being the allpowerful and unlimited fuel needed to travel the distance, and the Spiritual Gifts working in conjunction with God's Word is the directions and road map that shows the safest and most accurate path. One is necessary to make the car go; the other is necessary to make it travel in the right direction and, in the process, avoid all dangers and pitfalls one will encounter along the way. We are told that the path we must travel is narrow and we must "enter by the narrow gate; for wide is the gate and broad is the way that leads to destruction, and there are many who go in by it. Because narrow is the gate and difficult is the way which leads to life, and there are few who find it" (Matthew 7:13). We can only find that narrow path by using the Spiritual Gifts working in conjunction with God's Word, motivated and empowered by Love.

Although 1 Corinthians 13 gives us a definition, though unfinished, of what true godly love is, that is not the main emphasis of the chapter. Its main purpose is once again, to show us the relationship between Spiritual Gifts without Love and Spiritual Gifts with Love! Spiritual Gifts without Love or Love without Spiritual Gifts is the same as having all the fuel in the world without a map or having the best map without any fuel, both scenarios are useless for the journey ahead.

1 Corinthians 13 divides perfectly into three parts.

> First, we have Love Contrasted (verses 1-3). Though I speak with the tongues of men and of angels, but have not love, I have become sounding brass or a clanging cymbal. And though I have the gift of prophecy, and understand all mysteries and all knowledge, and though I have all faith, so that I could remove mountains, but have not love, I am nothing. And though I bestow all my goods to feed the poor, and though I give my body to be burned, but have not love, it profits me nothing.

Secondly, we have Love Analyzed (verses 4-8). Love suffers long and is kind, love does not envy; love does not parade itself, is not puffed up; does not behave rudely, does not seek its own, is not provoked, thinks no evil; does not rejoice in iniquity, but rejoices in the truth; bears all things, believes all things, hopes all things, endures all things.

Third we have Love Defended as Supreme (verses 9-13). Love never fails. But whether there are prophecies, they will fail; whether there are tongues, they will cease; whether there is knowledge, it will vanish away. For we know in part and we prophesy in part, but when that which is perfect has come, then that which is in part will be done away. When I was a child, I spoke as a child, I understood as a child, I thought as a child, but when I became a man, I put away childish things. For now, we see in a mirror, dimly, but then face to face. Now I know in part, but then I shall know just as I also am known. And now abide faith, hope, love, these three; but the greatest of these is love.

For many years, we have heard and been taught that the supreme attribute in the religious world was Faith. We would beg to differ. The supreme attribute of Christianity is the Love of God flowing in and through us. It is not an oversight that Paul who just a few moments before, speaking of faith said; "If I have all faith, so that I can remove mountains, and have not Love, I am nothing." And let us not forget that in verse 13 of 1 Corinthians he deliberately separates faith from love, "now abides faith, hope, love," and then he loudly declares, "The greatest of these is love."

1 Corinthian 13 does not stand alone in proclaiming that love

is the supreme good of Christianity. Other God inspired writers are agreed about it as well. Peter says, 'Above all things have fervent love among yourselves" (1 Peter 4:8). John goes even farther stating simply that "God is Love" (1 John 4:8). Do you remember the profound declaration that the former Pharisee Paul made about love? "Love is the fulfillment of the Law" (Romans 13:10b KJV).

Did you ever stop to think what was meant by that? Jesus gave us the meaning in Matthew 22:36-40 (KJV)

> "Master, which is the great commandment in the law?" Jesus said unto him, "Thou shalt love the Lord thy God with all thy heart, and with all thy soul, and with all thy mind. This is the first and great commandment. And the second is like unto it, thou shalt love thy neighbor as thyself. On these two commandments hang all the law and the prophets."

In other words, if we love God and man unconditionally, there is no need for the other commandments, but there is still a need for the Gifts, because the Gifts of God extend from God's love like fruit on a tree planted by God's living waters. The Spiritual Gifts working in conjunction with God's Word give us the shortest, fastest, and safest directions. They tell us which is the right way to go and which is not. Whereas, Love gives us the power and the fuel to help ourselves and others arrive in glory.

Keep in mind, in the first century AD. people believed that it was by the works of the law that they would make heaven their home. They had to strictly adhere to the original Ten Commandments plus a myriad of other commandments conceived in the mind of man. This belief was held by many church groups until Martin Luther nailed the 95 Theses to the door of the Castle Church in 1517, which began what is now known as the Protestant Reformation. The doctrine of salvation by works is still practiced and taught in some main line churches today. Christ showed us however, that love is the better way (refer Mark 12:28-34, especially verses 32-34). If we do not adhere to these impossible to satisfy commandments, but adhere to only one thing, love unconditionally, we will fulfill the whole law, and by faith in Christ, the way to Heaven will be open (Romans 1:17).

In other words, the man that truly loves his neighbor will not plot or do harm against him; he will not injure, nor defile his bed, nor rob or deceive, covet, or steal from him. He will not damage his character, bear false testimony against him, but, on the contrary, he will bestow upon him all the good he is capable of and in the same manner as he wishes to receive. Therefore, in love is the completion of all the requirements of the Law.

The Law meaning the Law of Moses generally speaking but specifically the Ten Commandments and even more specifically the second table of the Law (Commandments 5-10). This second table of the Law is described as man's actions toward man, or actions taken in regard to our duty to our neighbor. If people truly loved one another, all the demands of the Law would then be satisfied. Therefore, Love is the fulfilling of the law.

So how does the apostle Paul analyze Love? Love is the rule for fulfilling all rules, the new commandment for keeping all the old commandments. As stated earlier, when Jesus was asked about the greatest of all commandments, He responded by giving only two. Love is the essence of both! Love God above all. Love your neighbor as yourself. It couldn't be easier to understand. Understanding is one thing however; doing is another. Jesus made provision for that also. He said, "With men it is impossible, but not with God for with God all things are possible" (Mark 10:27). Moreover, the apostle Paul said, "I can do all things through Christ who strengthens me" (Philippians 4:13).

In verses 4-8 of 1 Corinthians 13, we have what might be described as the spectrum of Love, or the analysis of Love. Let's elements have common names. In fact, they are virtues that we hear about every day. They are things that can be practiced by every man at any time in life. The Spectrum of Love has nine ingredients:

1.	Patience	"Love suffers long."
2.	Kindness	"And is kind,"
3.	Generosity	"love envies not."
4.	Humility	"love does not parade itself, is not puffed up."
5.	Courtesy	"does not behave rudely."
6.	Unselfishness	"does not seek its own."
7.	Good Tempered	"is not easily provoked."
8.	Guilelessness	"thinks no evil."
9.	Sincerity	"rejoices not in iniquity, but rejoices in the truth."

These ingredients make up the supreme manifestation of Love, as well as the stature of the perfect man. You will observe that all these are related to men and to life. They all bear on the known today and the near tomorrow. They have no bearing at all on the unknown eternity. In eternity, there will be no suffering, unkindness, envy, or pride. There will only be love! In today's world and especially in today's churches, we hear much about loving God; however, Christ spoke much of loving man. We make much of peace in heaven, but Christ made much of peace on earth. Brethren, we need to get our priorities straight before we are called home or Christ returns. We must do as Paul in Philippians 2:5 said, "Let this mind be in you which was also in Christ Jesus." If we don't, we may not make heaven our home.

The supreme manifestation of Love is not a thing to be coveted, but a person, Jesus of Nazareth! Who was, is, and is to come? Who is the all in all, the Alpha and Omega, the beginning and the end? He is the one who from the beginning knew that man was evil and had no way of escaping the punishment due for his sin? Jesus is the one who knew that there was only one way for man to return to a place of rest and peace. He's the one who knew that man had no way of receiving the glory, honor, love, and acceptance that man once had with the Father of Lights. He's the one who, in His ultimate wisdom, recognized that there was no other way for His beloved creation to return to the loving bosom of God. Jesus knowing all this, and driven by His unlimited love for His creation, left all His Glory and came to earth as a servant and died as an eternal sacrifice in order to secure our return to fellowship with Him today and forever.

Jesus gave up the glories of heaven and the blessedness of His relationship with His Father so that God could use Him as a onetime sacrifice that would bridge the gulf between Himself and man.

> He who, being in the form of God, did not consider it robbery to be equal with God, but made Himself of no reputation, taking the form of a bondservant and coming in the likeness of men. And being found in appearance as a man, He humbled Himself and became obedient to the point of death, even the death of the cross.
>
> Philippians 2:6-8

The one and only true God, clothed with the mantle of mere man came with one solitary purpose. That divine purpose was the redemption of our souls. He did it by showing us what love really is. "For when we were still without strength, in due time Christ died for the ungodly. For scarcely for a righteous man will one die; yet perhaps, for a good man someone would even dare to die. But God demonstrates His own love toward us, in that while we were still sinners, Christ died for us" (Romans 5:6-8). And "by this we know love, because He laid down His life for us" (1 John 3:16a).

Is love the best way of obtaining all the Gifts God has to give His Bride? Absolutely! Without love, the Spiritual Gifts are like magnificent and powerful horses that are unbridled and untamed all pulling in different directions. The result is the king's chariot goes nowhere fast. The chariot and its horses as magnificent and beautiful as they are, become useless and ineffective for the journey ahead. Once these magnificent horses are harnessed to the King's chariot in love with the reins secured and placed into the hands of the King of Love, the chariot, which carries the magnificence of the King of Kings, will go forth in splendor, beauty, speed, and power. The King of Kings will then conquer all who would stand before Him.

Because of the pure and boundless love of God, the Church of Jesus Christ was given to mankind as a hospital for the sick, a shelter in the time of storm, a home to the homeless, and a source of strength to the weak. It is a place of provision to the poor, a deliverance center to the oppressed, a place of life to the dead, and a preservative to them that perish. The church is a place of faith to the faithless, hope to the hopeless, love to the unlovable. It is a place of knowledge to the unknowing, and a light to those who walk in the darkness of sin. It is a place of guidance for those who are lost, food for the hungry, water for the thirsty, and comfort to the comfortless. It is security to those in fear, and immovable for them who are tossed to and fro. How can we then succeed in being all God has called us to be without all the Spiritual and Administrative Gifts provided by God, which are empowered, and manifested by the Love of God, His divine and driving force. We can't!

Chapter Questions To
Help Your Study

1. 1 Corinthians 13 compares Spiritual Gifts without love and Spiritual Gifts with love. True or False
2. 1 Corinthians 13 divides into three parts. What are they?
3. 1 Corinthians 13 does not stand alone in proclaiming that love is the supreme good of Christianity. True or False
4. The Spectrum of Love has nine ingredients. What are they?

LOVE: PART ONE

I s Agape Love the best way of obtaining all the Gifts God has to give His Bride? Absolutely! If we believe that Agape Love is the all-powerful force that empowers, operates, inspires, and directs Spiritual Gifts, then it is vital that before we close our study on the Gifts of the Spirit, we must examine closely what is Love. We will examine the way John the Beloved described God's pure love. Then we will look at the magnificent gift that was brought to a lost and dying world, through God's pure love.

After prayerful consideration, however, we realized that the two subjects cannot be separated. When we study love, we have no other option then to study the magnificent gift that love brought. Beloved the two are in separable! Look once again at 1 John 3:16a; in which John states, "by this we know love, because he laid down his life for us." Why do we know love? Because He died for us! In this verse the "He" refers to Jesus the Christ. Look also at Romans 5:6-8, "For when we were still without strength, in due time Christ died for the ungodly. For scarcely for a righteous man will one die; yet perhaps for a good man someone would even dare to die. But God demonstrates His own love toward us, in that while we were still sinners, Christ died for us." In 1 John 4:9-10, John says, "In this the love of God was manifested toward us, that God has sent His only begotten Son into the world, that we might live through Him. In this is love not that we loved God but that He loved us and sent His Son to be the propitiation for our sins." And finally, John 3:16, which many Christians know well, Jesus said; "For God so loved the world that He gave His only begotten Son, that whoever believes in Him should not perish but have everlasting life." You cannot discuss the "Love of God" without discussing the action it prompted. Love can only be known by the action it prompts!

The main text for this study will be 1 John 4:7-21

> Beloved, let us love one another: for love is of God; and every one that loveth is born of God, and knows God. He who does not love does not know God, for God is love. In this the love of God was manifested toward us, that God has sent His only begotten Son into the world, that we might live through Him. In this is love, not that we loved God, but that He loved us and sent His Son to be the propitiation for our sins. Beloved, if God so loved us, we also ought to love one another. No one has seen God at any time. If we love one another, God abides in us, and His love has been perfected in us. By this we know that we abide in Him, and He in us, because He has given us of His Spirit. And we have seen and testify that the Father has sent the Son as Savior of the world. Whoever confesses that Jesus is the Son of God, God abides in him, and he in God. And we have known and believed the love that God has for us. God is love, and he who abides in love abides in God, and God in him. Love has been perfected among us in this: that we may have boldness in the Day of Judgment; because as He is, so are we in this world. There is no fear in love; but perfect love casts out fear, because fear involves torment. But he who fears has not been made perfect in love. We love Him because He first loved us. If someone says, "I love God," and hates his brother, he is a liar; for he who does not love his brother whom he has seen, how can he love God

whom he has not seen? And this commandment
we have from Him: that he who loves God must
love his brother also.

First, let's look at verses 8 and 16. Repeated twice, one time in
each verse, the same phrase appears; "God is Love." The Greek word
is agape. Agape is the noun. Agape the noun and its corresponding
verb "agapao" are never and can never be translated as loving. In
these verses, we see it translated the only way it can be translated
accurately, God is Love." If it was rendered "God is loving" (once
again, it is not translated like this in any version of the Bible), it
would make God a being that had an attribute of Love. Love would
then be just a part of His being, not His very nature, essence, and
existence. If love was only a part of His being, how could we have
faith and trust in Him? Because there would always be the doubt
of how God would react to us in any given situation, or for that
matter, would He react at all? But because His nature, His essence,
His being, and His very existence "is "love, there can be no doubt
to how He will react in every situation and in every action He
takes. God can only react in Love! He can only react in love, for it
is an extension of His divine nature. Love is not drawn out of God
because of the excellence of an object. God's Love is not complacent
or passive; it is the driving force behind His actions.

Love can only be known by the actions it prompts!

In fact, it is so important that man understands the truth of
God's love that God made love the Alpha and Omega of His Word.
Love is the golden thread that runs throughout the entire Bible. It
starts with God expressing His love to man in the creation story of
Genesis, where all things were made for man and man was made
for God. It showed itself even further with man being created in the
image and likeness of God. It then demonstrates itself throughout
man's history by God's repeated restoration of His creation from

depravity and sin. Then it reaches its zenith at the sacrificial death of God Himself in human flesh on the cross of Calvary. The story of God's Love does not end there however. Its absolute fullness will be revealed and seen face to face when the heavens are opened, and Jesus returns to rule and reign forever.

Agape is the expression of a perfect, Holy being to an imperfect, unholy, sinful, and unworthy mankind whose righteousness is like filthy rags before God (Isaiah 64:6). Its expression produces a reverential love in man toward God the giver, "We love [Him] because He first loved us" (1 John 4:19). This love relationship reveals itself by loving all mankind.

> Beloved, if God so loved us, we also ought to love one another...If we love one another, God abides in us, and His love has been perfected in us. If someone says, "I love God," and hates his brother, he is a liar, for he who does not love his brother whom he has seen, how can he love God whom he has not seen? And this commandment we have from Him: that he who loves God must love his brother also.
>
> 1 John 4: 11-12, 20-21

Practical love toward others, enables man to seek the Giver of Love, the one who is love, God Himself (Romans 15:2, 2 Corinthians 5:18-20). Practical love's perfect expression and perfect operation were seen through the birth, life, and death of the only begotten of the Father, Jesus the Christ (John 3:16, Romans 5:8, 8:32-39, 2 Corinthians 5:14, Ephesians 2:4, 5:2, and others).

Let us further examine love referencing 1 John 4:7, John 3:16 and 1 John 4:9.

Beloved, let us love one another, for love is of God; and everyone who loves is born of God and knows God.

1 John 4:7

For God so loved the world that He gave His only begotten Son, that whoever believes in Him should not perish but have everlasting life.

John 3:16

In this the love of God was manifested toward us, that God has sent His only begotten Son into the world, that we might live through Him

1 John 4:9

We see in these verses listed below, God's Love commanded, translated, and demonstrated.

1. God 'commanded" us to walk in Love toward one another (1 John 4:7), just as Christ loved us and given Himself for us (Ephesians 5:2).
2. God's Love was "translated" to us in His Son, who came as a man to show us the Fathers Love (John 3:16; Romans 5:6-8; Galatians 4:4-5)
3. God then "demonstrated" that love when he died on Calvary's cross so that we might live through Him (1 Thessalonians 5:9-10; 1 John 4:9).

Let us illustrate what has been observed so far.

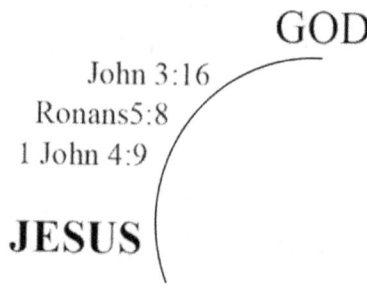

GOD

John 3:16
Ronans5:8
1 John 4:9

JESUS

Let's look again at 1 John 4:9. "In this the love of God was manifested toward us, that God has sent His only begotten Son into the world, that we might live through Him." God manifested His love to man in His Son's death on Calvary. Let's look at the words of this verse a little closer. The word manifested, means to demonstrate or to show, to exhibit openly, to cause to shine forth, to make visible. God manifested His love in an open spectacle or display. God made an open display of His only begotten Son, by hanging Him in midair, with His hands and feet nailed to a cross (John 19: 16-19). What is even more profound is that "God demonstrated His love in that while we were yet sinners, Christ died for us" (Romans 5:8).

The cross was placed on the top of a hill called Calvary or in Hebrew Golgotha, which means the "Place of the Skull." This place of execution was in a public location so all could see the spectacle. He hung there for three hours while people gawked, and scorned at His bloodied, torn, naked, and beaten body as it hung on that cross. He was there to take away the sins of the world, and to free all mankind from eternal punishment. He hung there to give eternal life to anyone that believes in Him. He made a way for a sinful world, which otherwise would have no hope of ever seeing God's loving face, to return home to the loving bosom of their Father in Heaven. How little they knew. "And I, if I am lifted up from the earth, will draw all peoples to myself." This he said, signifying by what death he would die. (Ref. John 12:32-33).

Therefore remember that you, once Gentiles in the flesh who are called Uncircumcision by what is called the Circumcision made in the flesh by hands, that at that time you were without Christ, being aliens from the commonwealth of Israel and strangers from the covenants of promise, having no hope and without God in the world. But now in Christ Jesus you who once were far off have been brought near by the blood of Christ. For He Himself is our peace, who has made both one, and has broken down the middle wall of separation, having abolished in His flesh the enmity, that is, the law of commandants contained in ordinances, so as to create in Himself one new man from the two, thus making peace, and that He might reconcile them both to God in one body through the cross, thereby putting to death the enmity.

Ephesians 2:11-16

This act of Agape (God's Love) accomplished four wonderful and eternal accomplishments accessible to whoever comes to the cross in faith. These four accomplishments are:

1. Propitiation
2. Redemption
3. Justification
4. Reconciliation

Let's look a little closer at these four blessings Christ's sacrifice brought.

Propitiation (hisaskomai) mean to appease or pacify anger. If we are to develop truly Biblical doctrine of propitiation, it will be necessary to look at three points concerning propitiation:

1. why propitiation is necessary,

2. who made it,
3. and what the propitiation was.

First, propitiation focuses on the wrath of God directed toward man because of man's disobedience. Disobedience is sin! Sin arouses the wrath of God, this wrath brings the judgment of God upon the sinner, "for the wages of sin is death; but the gift of God is eternal life through Jesus Christ our Lord." (Romans 6:23). This is why propitiation is necessary.

> He who believes in the Son has everlasting life; and he who does not believe on the son of God shall not see life, but the wrath of God abides on him.
>
> John 3:36

> For the wrath of God is revealed from heaven against all ungodliness and unrighteousness of men, who suppress the truth in unrighteousness...
>
> Romans 1:18

> ...therefore, put to death your members which are on the earth: fornication, uncleanness, passion, evil desire, and covetousness, which is idolatry. Because of these things the wrath of God is coming upon the sons of disobedience.
>
> Colossians 3:5-6

Second, who makes the propitiation? Propitiation is never used of any act whereby man brings God into a favorable attitude or gracious disposition, but always used in relation to all actions taken by God whereby He brings man into a favorable relationship with Himself. It is God who is propitiated (appeased or satisfied) through the provision He made in the sacrifice of His only Son. God has so dealt with sin that He can show mercy to a believing sinner in the removal of all his guilt and the remission of all his sins. The primary principle on which God deals with sinners is expressed in the words "apart from shedding of blood," unless a death takes place, "there is no remission of sins" (Hebrews 9:22).

Let's look at a few verses that will help us to further answer the question, who makes the propitiation?

> For the life of the flesh is in the blood, and I have given it to you upon the altar to make atonement for your souls; for it is the blood that makes atonement for the soul.
>
> Leviticus 17:11

> ...whom God set forth as a propitiation by His blood, through faith, to demonstrate His righteousness, because in His forbearance God had passed over the sins that were previously committed.
>
> Romans 3:25

> In this is love, not that we loved God, but that He God loved us and sent His Son to be the propitiation for our sins.
>
> 1 John 4:10

P. T. Forsyth expresses the act of propitiation like this, "the atonement [Christ's sacrificial death] did not procure grace. It flowed from grace."[41] God does not love us because Christ died for us; Christ died for us because God loved us! If it is God's wrath that needed to be propitiated, it is God's love that did the propitiating. Let us be clear. It was not propitiation that changed God's wrath to love or our sin that changed God's love to wrath. God's nature is unchanging. What the propitiation changed was the way God deals with mankind. "The distinction I ask you to observe," wrote

P. T. Forsyth, "is between a change of feeling and a change of treatment...God's feeling toward us never needed to be changed. But God's treatment of us, God's practical relation to us that had to change."[42]

Third, what was the propitiatory sacrifice? It was neither an animal, nor a vegetable, nor a mineral. It was not a thing at all, but a person. The person God offered was not somebody who was distinct from or external to Himself. No, He offered Himself. He gave His only begotten Son. Look once again at John 4:10, "In this is love, not that we loved God, but that He (God) loved us and sent His Son to be the propitiation for our sins."

So then, God Himself is at the heart of the answer to all three questions regarding propitiation. It was God Himself who because of His Holy wrath toward man's sinfulness, needed to be propitiated. God Himself who in holy love for His creation undertook the propitiating, and God Himself who in the person of His Son sacrificed Himself for that propitiation. In other words, God out of His nature of love took the initiative to appease His own righteous anger by bearing the act of propitiation upon Himself, through the atonement of His son, Jesus. Jesus suffered and died so we did not have to.

Redemption. While propitiation focuses on the wrath of God, which was appeased by the cross, redemption focuses on the plight of sinners from which they were ransomed by the cross. Ransomed is the correct word. The Greek words "lytroo" (usually translated as redeem) and "apolytrosis" (redemption) are derived from the word "lytron" (a ransom or the price of release), which was almost a technical term in the ancient world for the purchase or formal releasing of a slave. Warfield explains redemption by saying, "A redemption without a price paid is as anomalous (unusual) a transaction as a sale without money passing."[43]

Redemption encompasses three important parts:

1. The desperate plight of the sinner.

2. The price needed to purchase our freedom.
3. The person who did the redeeming.

Let's look at some verses that show us the desperate plight of the sinner.

Sinners are Spiritually Dead.

> "but of the tree of the knowledge of good and evil you shall not eat, for in the day that you eat of it you shall surely die."
>
> Genesis 2:17

> "But he who sins against me wrongs his own soul; All those who hate me love death."
>
> Proverbs 8:36

> Ezekiel 18:4 "Behold, all souls are Mine; The soul of the father as well as the soul of the son is Mine; The soul who sins shall die." (Refer also to James 1:15 and 5:20.)

Sinners are Separated from God.

> But your iniquities have separated you from your God; and your sins have hidden His face from you, so that He will not hear.
>
> Isaiah 59:2

> But now in Christ Jesus you who once were far off have been brought near by the blood of Christ. For He Himself is our peace, who has made both one, and has broken down the middle wall of separation, having abolished in His flesh the enmity, that is, the law of commandments contained in ordinances, so

as to create in Himself one new man from the two, thus making peace, and that He might reconcile them both to God in one body through the cross, thereby putting to death the enmity. And He came and preached peace to you who were afar off and to those who were near.

Ephesians 2:13-18

Sinners have no Means of Escaping the Curse on their own.

How shall we escape if we neglect so great a salvation, which at the first began to be spoken by the Lord, and was confirmed to us by those who heard Him.

Hebrews 2:3

See that you do not refuse Him who speaks. For if they did not escape who refused Him who spoke on earth, much more shall we not escape if we turn away from Him who speaks from heaven.

Hebrews 12:25

What was the price of our redemption? To begin with, there was the cost of the incarnation. God gave up eternity and all the glories of heaven and entered into our human condition as a servant (Philippians 2). We are told that when God sent His Son, He was "born under the law, to redeem those under the law" (Galatians 4:4, 5).

Then there was the cost of the atonement. To accomplish this, He gave "Himself' or His "life," dying under the law's curse to redeem us from it.

"Christ has redeemed us from the curse of the law, having become a curse for us (for it is written, "Cursed is everyone who hangs on a tree),"

Galatians 3:13

"For even the Son of Man did not come to be served, but to serve, and to give His life a ransom for many."

Mark 10:45

"For if when we were enemies we were reconciled to God through the death of His Son, much more, having been reconciled, we shall be saved by His life." (Also refer to Ephesians 1:7, and Titus 2:4.)

Romans 5:10

Finally, it was the person who did the redeeming. We have already seen that Jesus was the person that did the redeeming. Therefore, the act of paying our ransom by His own death gives Him exclusive rights over His purchase. Thus, Jesus' lordship is directly attributed to our plight and the price He paid to obtain our release. If we were worth the cost, is He not worth our labor?

The privilege of serving Him is established by the preciousness of the price paid for our purchase. That is why we read that the community in heaven sings His praises continually.

And they sang a new song, saying: "You are worthy to take the scroll, and to open its seals; for You were slain, and have redeemed us to God by Your blood Out of every tribe and tongue and people and nation.

Revelation 5:9

They sang as it were a new song before the throne, before the four living creatures, and the elders; and no one could learn that song except the hundred and fortyfour thousand who were redeemed from the earth. These are the ones who were not defiled with women, for they are virgins. These are the ones who follow the Lamb wherever He goes. These were redeemed from among men, being first fruits to God and to the Lamb.

Revelation 14:3-4

Just to reiterate what has been said because it is so very important to do so, the Lord Jesus Christ has purchased our salvation with His life, and as a result we belong to Him. Should this not motivate us as individual Christians to strive to obtain holiness, and to give Him all praise and worship, in the same way that it motivates the heavenly host to do the same? Ask yourself; is He not worth my holiness and my worship? Next, we will look at what Justification and Reconciliation are, the command to love, and the standard we are to live by. We will also examine the inward and outward evidence of love and the result of loving.

Chapter Questions To Help Your Study

1. Love can only be known by what?
2. Agape (noun) and its corresponding verb, "Agapao" is never, and can never be translated what?
3. Agape is the expression of a perfect, holy being to an imperfect, unholy, sinful, and unworthy mankind. True or False
4. In 1st John 4:7, John 3:16, and 1 Thessalonians 5:9-10 we see God's Love, _____

   _____

   _____

   _____

   _____

   _____

5. This act of Agape (God's Love) gave four wonderful and eternal things to whomever comes to the cross in faith. What are they?
6. Redemption encompasses three important parts. What are they?
7. What three things can be said about the plight of sinners?
8. What was the price of our redemption?

LOVE: PART TWO

There is logic in the order in which we are reviewing these great words, which describe the magnificent accomplishments of the cross. First is Propitiation. Propitiation inevitably comes first because until the wrath of God is appeased (that is, until His love has found a way to avert His anger) there can be no redemption.

Second is redemption. Redemption means to be rescued from the   grim judgment of sin, which comes only through the atonement, which came at a high price, Christ's blood.

Third is Justification. Justification, through the sin cleansing blood, bestows on us a right standing before God. My sins no longer keep me from God.

Fourth is Reconciliation, which brings adoption and unrestricted access to our heavenly Father.

The two pictures we have so far considered have led us into the temple precincts (Propitiation), because that is where we must go to appease the wrath of God. And the market place (Redemption), where the price for our freedom from sin was paid. The third image (Justification) will take us into the courthouse, for justification is the opposite of condemnation (Romans 5:18, 8:34). Both are verdicts of a judge who pronounces the accused either guilty or not guilty. Justification signifies pronouncing one righteous or to acquit one of guilt.

Its precise meaning is determined by that of the verb "dikaioo," which means to justify. It is used only twice in the New Testament, both in the epistle to the Romans (4:25, 5:18). They signify the establishment of a person as just by acquittal from guilt. In Romans 4:25 the phrase "for our justification," which is literally translated "because of our justification," simply means that whatsoever was necessary for God to do in order to establish our justification, God accomplished through the death of His only begotten Son. Put simply, justification means, "Christ took our place while we took His."

Let us look again at our illustration.

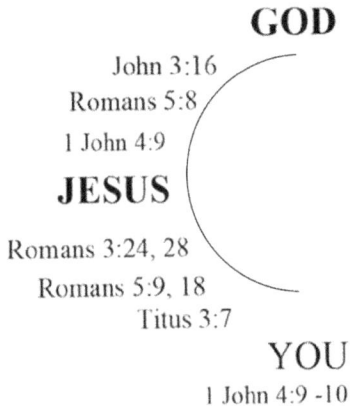

GOD

John 3:16
Romans 5:8
1 John 4:9

JESUS

Romans 3:24, 28
Romans 5:9, 18
Titus 3:7

YOU
1 John 4:9 -10

The fourth image of salvation, which illustrates the achievement of the cross, is Reconciliation. John R. W. Stott, a British Christian leader and Anglican clergyman. A man noted as a leader of the worldwide evangelical movement, and an author of fifty books on Christian Theology explains reconciliation as probably the most popular of the four magnificent results of the atonement, because it is the most personal.

> We have left behind the temple precincts, the market place, and the law court; we are now in our own home with our family and friends. There is a quarrel true enough, even enmity, but to reconcile means to restore a relationship, to renew a friendship. This fact presupposes and original relationship was enjoyed. That former relationship with God

having been broken sometime in the past, has been recovered by Christ.[44]

The Greek word used for reconciliation is "katallasso" a verb. It properly denotes a change or to exchange (for a price). In regard to mankind, it means to change from enmity to friendship or to reconcile with the one offended. In regard to the relationship between God and man, reconciliation is that which only God can accomplish by God exercising His grace so that prodigal mankind can come home to his once orphaned family. The foundation for reconciliation was the death of Christ in a propitiatory sacrifice under the judgment of sin (2 Corinthians 5:19). By reason of this propitiatory sacrifice, men in their sinful condition and alienation from God are invited to reconcile, that is to say, to change their attitude and accept the provision God has made, whereby their sins can be remitted and they themselves justified in the sight in God

Reconciliation is not a term the Bible uses to describe "coming to terms with oneself," although it does insist that it is only by losing oneself in love for God and neighbor that we truly find ourselves. Reconciliation with God means to come to terms with God based upon God's precepts. Reconciliation can only become a reality by Atonement. Atonement alludes to the event through which God and human beings, previously alienated from one another, are reconciled or made "at one" again. Let us take a moment to cover a few important facts about Atonement.

1. Atonement is the means, whereas Reconciliation is the result.
2. Atonement does not procure Grace; it was Grace that procured the Atonement.
3. God does not love us because Christ died for us, but Christ died for us because God loved us, thereby giving us the Atonement.

4. It was God's wrath that needed appeasement, and God's Love, which did the appeasing. The Atonement was the means in which God obtained appeasement.

5. The price of the Atonement was the death of God's only Son (Romans 5:10).

Now, back to reconciliation! Romans 5:9-11, is one of the four great passages on reconciliation in the New Testament, in this passage to be reconciled and to be justified are paralleled.

> Being now justified by his blood, we shall be saved from wrath through him. For if, while we were enemies, we were reconciled to God by the death of his Son, much more, being reconciled, we shall be saved by his life. And not only so, but we also joy in God through our Lord Jesus Christ, by whom we have now received the atonement.

Notice, "being now justified by his blood" is paralleled by the word "if." "For if: while we were enemies, we were reconciled to God by the death of his Son, much more, being reconciled, we shall be saved by his life". Notice the state of man, one needing justification, the other reconciliation; though both are affected by the cross, they are not identical. Where justification is our legal standing before our judge in a court of law, reconciliation is our personal relationship with our Father in the home. The latter is the sequel and fruit of the former. It is only when we have been justified by faith that we have peace with God as our Father in heaven that is reconciliation (Romans 5:1).

Whenever in God's Word the verb "to reconcile" appears, either God or Man is the object, God reconciles or man is reconciled. God is never the subject; God is not the one reconciled. God was never and will never have to be reconciled to us; it is always God or God through Christ reconciling us to Himself!

There are two other terms that confirm the fact that reconciliation means peace with God adoption and access. With regard to the former, John, who attributes our being children of God to our being born of God, expresses his sense of wonder that the Father loved us enough to make us, His children (John 1:12-13, 1 John 3:1-10). In regard to the latter, Paul twice places "access to God" and "peace with God" together. The first time attributing them to our justification (Romans 5:1-2), and the second time explaining "access" as a Trinitarian experience (Ephesians 2:17-22). We have access to the Father through the Son by the Spirit Putting it simply, through reconciliation we are adopted into God's family, we are His children, and we have unrestrictive access to the Father and may approach our Heavenly Father at any time we wish with freedom and confidence (Ephesians 3:12).

Reconciliation also has a horizontal as well as a vertical effect, for God has reconciled us into His new family, as well as to Himself. Another great New Testament passage focuses on these effects (Ephesians 2:11-22). He reminds His Gentile Christian readers that formerly they were on the one hand excluded from citizenship in Israel and foreigners to the covenants of promise and on the other "separate from Christ...and without God in the world" (verse 12). As Gentiles we were "far away," separated, or alienated from God and from Israel. In this passage the term Gentiles is used as a metaphor for heathens or unbelievers and Israel a metaphor for the people of promise, people who accept the conditions of the promise and therefore have received the promise. We Gentiles were doubly alienated, "but now in Christ Jesus," Paul goes on to say, "you who once were far away (Gentiles) have been brought near through the blood of Christ" (verse 13). In fact, Christ, who "Himself is our peace," has broken down the barrier of separation between Jew and Gentile, and "made the two one" (verse 14). Christ's atonement has both "abolished" the law which kept the two apart, but "created" in Himself "one new man [believers] out of the two, thus making peace" (verse 15, word in Parenthesis added).

These are the four great accomplishments that God's love brought the human race, but love is not perfected by the effects created by these four great accomplishments alone. How can they be; if the world does not know or is not told about them? Let's look at Romans 10:13-17, 2 Corinthians 3:2 and 1 John 4:12, for more clarification.

> "For whoever calls on the name of the LORD shall be saved." How then shall they call on Him in whom they have not believed? And how shall they believe in Him of whom they have not heard? And how shall they hear without a preacher? And how shall they preach unless they are sent? As it is written: "How beautiful are the feet of those who preach the gospel of peace, who bring glad tidings of good things!" But they have not all obeyed the gospel. For Isaiah said, "Lord, who has believed our report?" So, then faith comes by hearing, and hearing by the word of God."
>
> Romans 10:13-17

> You are our epistle written in our hearts, known and read by all men.
>
> 1 John 4:12

> No one has seen God at any time. If we love one another, God abides In us, and His love has been perfected in us."
>
> 2 Corinthians 3:2

According to these verses, especially 1 John 4:12, God's love is not perfected "in us" if we do not love one another. His work becomes non effective if the world is not told about the tremendous love of God that brought forth His Son to reconcile us back to the

Father. What exactly does it mean that Love cannot be perfected in us? Is not Agape Love perfect? Yes, Agape Love is perfect! For Agape is the nature of God Himself. However, it is not perfect "in us" if we do not love others the same way God loves us and gave His life for a ransom for many.

Beloved we stop God's love from being fulfilled in the world and in us when we take our newfound relationship with Him and keep it to ourselves. Remember "for God so loved the world (you are included in the world but not alone in it), that He gave His only begotten son" (John 3:16). Read again the verses above, how will they know, how will they hear unless we tell them. Why? Because you [we] are the epistles written in our hearts, known, and read by all men (1 John 4:12). Paul put it this way,

> How then shall they call on him in whom they have not believed? And how shall they believe in him of whom they have not heard? And how shall they hear without a preacher? And how shall they preach, except they be sent? As it is written, how beautiful are the feet of them that preach the gospel of peace, and bring glad tidings of good things.
>
> Romans 10:13-15

Once we receive the pure and undefiled love of God in our hearts, we, by keeping it to ourselves, defile it. We take away its perfection. Just like living water dies and becomes polluted when it stagnates so does the pure and holy love of God when, by stopping it from an outlet, we stagnate it. Living water must flow outward, be absorbed, and by absorption, it will produce life.

To that end, God starts a work in us called Sanctification. Sanctification means to be set apart for God's use. The process of Sanctification is the process in which God removes our sin and purifies our natures so that the same godly love that was received and placed within us at our conversion becomes, once again as it began, Pure and Holy in us and in the world around us through the ministry of reconciliation (2 Corinthians 5:18).

To be perfected means to become mature or to bring one to fullness. That fullness can only be in Christ. This perfection only comes from inspecting one's own self in the pure true light of God's Holy Word, with the help of and through the power of the Holy Spirit.

Brethren we must realize that bringing the true light of God's love to the world is a major part of that process. Understanding this makes it easy to see that loving God and loving others are inseparable (1 John 4:21). Let's take a closer look at 1 John 4:21-5:1.

And this commandment we have from Him: that he who loves God must love his brother also. Whoever believes that Jesus is the Christ is born of God, and everyone who loves Him who begot also loves him who is begotten of Him.

First, the Command:
And this commandment we have from Him: that he who loves God must love his brother also.

Second, the Standard:
Whoever believes that Jesus is the Christ is born of God, and everyone who loves Him who begot also loves him who is begotten of Him. The New American Standard Bible puts it this way,
"Whoever believes that Jesus is the Christ is born of God, and everyone who loves the Father loves the child born of Him. By this we know that we love the children of God, when we love God and observe His commandments."

Now read again 2 Corinthians 3:2 in which Paul writes to the church of Corinth, "You are our epistle written in our hearts, known and read by all men."

Mankind will not know the love of God unless each member of the body of Christ shows forth God's love the same way Christ did in word and in work. So, shall we. Look at Matthew 28:18-20, Mark 16:15, Luke 24:47, John 21:15-17, and Acts 1:8. Do you see a recurring theme? Go preach the Gospel the good news of God's love, to the world, in word and work!

Let us once again continue with our illustration of what we have seen so far.

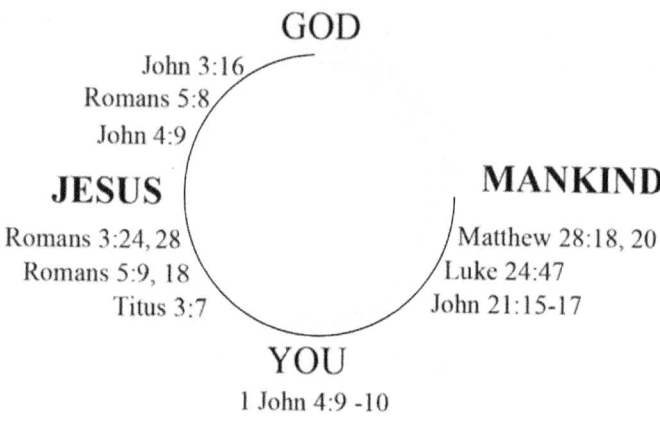

God's Love, His nature and His being, was manifested in His Son Jesus Christ. It was demonstrated by His sacrificial death so that sinful man could be brought back into the presence of the Almighty, becoming adopted heirs and Sons of the Father. With this privilege comes the command to share the love of God with others so that God's love can be perfected in us. We are told to go into the entire world and preach the Gospel by word, work, and by our lifestyle. This perfecting can easily be seen in 1 John 4:17 which says, "Love has been perfected among us in this: that we may have boldness in the Day of Judgment; because as He is, so are we in this world." He was and still is the personification of Love manifested in the Gifts this book is dedicated to educate us on, and inspire us to use. Along with this read these verses: 2 Corinthians 5: 18-21 and 1 John 4:13-15. They show us the pure God given definition of God's love. Let's look at these verses together.

> Now all things are of God, who has reconciled us to Himself through Jesus Christ, and has given us the ministry of reconciliation, that is, that God was in Christ reconciling the world to Himself; not imputing their trespasses to them, and has committed to us the word of reconciliation. Now then, we are ambassadors for Christ, as though God were pleading through us: we implore you on Christ's behalf, be reconciled to God. For He made Him who knew no sin to be sin for us, that we might become the righteousness of God in Him.
>
> 2 Corinthians 5:18-21

> By this we know that we abide in Him, and He in us, because He has given us of His Spirit. And we have seen and testify that the Father has sent the Son as Savior of the world. Whoever confesses that Jesus is the Son of God, God abides in him, and he in God.
>
> 1 John 4:13-15

Allow me to illustrate the main points of what was just said by placing them in list form.

1. The inward evidence of our salvation is the Spirit of God.
2. The outward evidence of our salvation is our testimony of Jesus as the savior of our souls and of the world.
3. The result of this salvation is that we abide in Him and He abides in us.

In conclusion let us review Matthew 22:36-40

"Teacher, which is the great commandment in the law?" Jesus said to him, "You shall love the LORD your God with all your heart, with all your soul, and with all your mind. This is the first and great commandment. And the second is like it: You shall love your neighbor as yourself. On these two command ments hang all the Law and the Prophets."

What are the commands?

1. Love God
2. Love Man

The word for love in these verses, in the Greek is "Agapao." This is the verb form of the word Agape. This means, we must love in action not in word alone.

These two commands are inseparable. On these two lay all the Law and the Prophets, the fulfillment of all of God's work, His entire Word, all Christ is, and all He came and died for. On these two commands, Love God and Love Man, rests all. It is the foundation of the largest building ever created; without these two foundational pillars, everything is laid waste. To what end are these two great commands given? The end is to bring a fallen sinful creation, loved by God above all others, back to the outstretched arms of a loving Creator, who is ever longing for their return. So, He can bring them from Glory to Glory until finally we are complete and perfect in Him.

In these two commands, God's Love was made complete. God's love starts with God who is Love. It is manifested in Christ who is the fulfillment and perfect image of the Father. Who came to earth to serve His creation and die for their sin, because they were helpless to escape the wages of that sin on their own? This opened up a pathway back to the Father so that we can abide with Him once more. Finally, to complete and make perfect that love, we are told to go and tell others of His love, demonstrate His nature, and manifest His Gifts so that the world can become as we are, adopted heirs with perfect and complete access to the Father of all. God's love is a complete and perfect circle. If we break that circle at any point Agape love, God's love, becomes incomplete, imperfect, and void of purity. It ceases to be Agape!

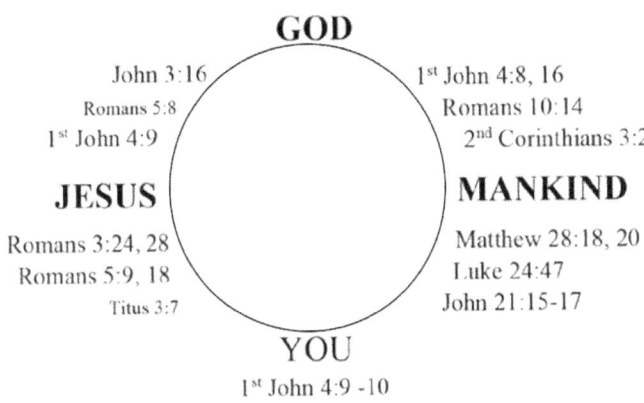

Brethren, with a pure and honest heart I present this one last truth. This truth is not novel, just forgotten or overlooked in the light of the outward glory and majesty of the Gifts. It has always been God's ultimate goal and primary purpose for His creation. It was foreknown and predestined in the heart of God before the world began. It has never changed! It has never wavered! Every gift of God, every aspect of God's being, every action ever taken on His part, every guideline, commandment, teaching, everything given to man that came from the Father of Lights, has been for the obtaining of this one sole purpose.

We can see it plainly declared in the first book of His Word with the creation of man. We see it in the first prophecy (Genesis 3:15), we see it throughout the History books in God's relationship and provision for a fallen creation. We see it in His laws and precepts. We see it loudly proclaimed in musical worship. We see it in the cries of God's prophets. We see it manifested and unveiled in the birth of God's only begotten Son, Jesus. We see it throughout the instructions found in the New Testament Epistles. We see it in His Gifts, and finally we see it revealed in the last book of the Bible, Revelation.

The foreknown and predestinated goal of God's heart was and is to create man in His own image. God wants us to reclaim that which was lost due to sin. Man remade in God's image. That is, it, brethren. Man made in God's image. This is, always has been, and always will be the heart of God. It should be the ultimate desire of all mankind as well; we must yearn to be changed into God's image.

In Romans 8:28-29 Paul declares this truth plainly, openly, and succinctly. It is unmistakable!

> And we know that all things work together for good to them that love God, to them who are the called according to his purpose. For whom he did foreknow, he also did predestinate to be conformed to the image of his Son, that he might be the firstborn among many brethren.

Refer also to these other verses: Romans 13:14; John 17:16, 19, 22-23, 26; 1 Corinthians 15:49; 2 Corinthians 3:18; Ephesians 1:4: 4:15, 24; Philippians 3:21;1 John 3:2.

Whom did God foreknow? God foreknew those that would love Him. God before time was even created looked into eternity and saw those that would love Him. He foreknew. Those that He foreknew, He predestinated. He did not predestinate them to love or hate God, not even that they should believe or not believe, nor that some should be saved and others damned, nor to claim our rightful place in heaven. No, my brethren! These are mere byproducts of a loving God.

Those whom God saw down through the annals of time, who would love Him; He predestinated for only one ultimate and magnificent purpose. They that love Him should be conformed into the image of His Son. The only thing predestinated, or foreordained, is that those who love God as revealed in Christ shall become Christ like in life, and like Christ in eternity.

To be conformed to the image of His Son, means to be made like unto our Lord Jesus in affection and disposition, in life and conversation, in the temper of our minds, and in the actions of our lives. It means to be like Him in His sufferings, and in the source of all His sufferings. It means to be like Him through the same kind of sufferings, like reproach, hatred, outward violence, and even death itself if need be, and do it with the same characteristics He demonstrated through those sufferings. If we let Him demonstrate through our sufferings, faith in word and work, love for the Father as well as all mankind, meekness, patience, and absolute assurance of our promised end, we shall be glorified. We will be like unto Him in all His Glory.

An unknown composer wrote a song that describes the goal of God's heart. The essence of the words of this small song should be the earnest longing of our hearts.

> *To be like Jesus*
> *To be like Jesus*
> *All I ask is to be like Him*
> *All through life's journey*
> *From earth to Glory*
> *All I ask is to be like Him*

I hope that this study on the Gifts of the Spirit have been a blessing to you. I pray that it has encouraged you to seek the Gifts for the edification, purification, and maturing of the saints. Moreover, I desire that the Gifts may work in you to accomplish God's ultimate purpose, making all mankind into the image of Christ. I pray that all of you have seen the necessity for these Gifts in the world today. And how these Gifts when used properly and with the propelling power of God's love can easily change individual lives, homes, churches, ministries, communities, governments, local, statewide, and national, and thereby change the world around us.

Continue to pray for these Gifts to operate in you and in your church. Allow God to demonstrate His love toward you and those with whom you come in contact. Use these Gifts to help bring lost souls to salvation, to repair broken spirits, heal diseased bodies, and give comfort to those who mourn. Let these God ordained Gifts help bring life to the dead and peace to those filled with fear. Our God is a God of today. He is filled with answers for all of today's questions. Let Him be the Lord of your life. Let Him use you in any way He wants to. For it is our solemn responsibility to look for opportunities to be used by God. Remember, God is not looking for ability but for availability. Pray that you become totally available to God. Remember what Paul wrote in 2 Corinthians 3:2, "You are the epistle written in our hearts known and read by all men."

Chapter Questions To
Help Your Study

1. Justification is the opposite of condemnation. True of False
2. Justification denotes the act of pronouncing righteous, or acquittal. True or False
3. Justification means "Christ took our place while we
4. The Greek word used for reconciliation is "katallasso" a verb. It denotes what?
5. Atonement alludes to the event through which God and human beings, previously alienated from one another, and now made one again. True or False
6. What are a few important facts about Atonement?

May God richly bless you.
In His love and service
Your Brother in Christ,

Rev. Mario A. Bruni D Div.

BIBLIOGRAPHY

I would like to acknowledge the magnificent authors and their works referred to in the preparation of this material. Many of these mighty men of God are far more learned and experienced than I. Their materials have been a source of much wisdom and understanding in which I used to write this humble work.

1. The Morning Star Journal, Rick Joyner, Morning Star Publications, Volume 3, No.2, 3, 4; Volume 4, No. 1; Volume 5, No. 2 Volume 7, No. 2, 3, 4; Volume 8, No. 2, 3; Volume 9, No. 2. 1998-1999.
2. Ungers Bible Dictionary, Moody Press, 1987.
3. The New Lexicon Webster's Dictionary of the English Language, Encyclopedic Edition, Lexicon Publications, Inc. 1998.
4. The New Strong's Exhaustive Concordance of the Bible, James Strong, LL.D., S.T.D., Thomas Nelson Publications, 1984.
5. Young's Analytical Concordance of the Bible, Robert Young, LL.D., Wm. B. Eerdmans Publishing Co., April 1977.
6. Matthew Henry's Commentary, Matthew Henry, MacDonald Publishing, 1706
7. Jamison, Fausset, & Brown, a Commentary, Critical, Experimental, and Practical, Wm. B. Eerdmans Publishing Co., 1973.

8. Romans, Donald Grey Barnhouse, Wm. B. Eerdmans Publishing Co., 1983.

9. Commentary of 1st Corinthians, Godet, Kregel Publications', 1977.

10. The Holy Spirit and His Gifts, Kenneth E. Hagin, Faith Library Publications, 1991.

11. The More Excellent Way, Dr. Mitch Medina, Paraclete Ministries Press, 1991.

12. Tongues, Interpretation, & Prophecy, Don Basham, Whitaker House, 1971.

13. The Gifts of the Spirit, Harold Horton, Radiant Books, Gospel Publishing House, 1975.

14. Ever Increasing Faith, Smith Wigglesworth, Gospel Publishing House, Revised edition, June 1971.

15. The First Epistle of Paul to the Corinthians, The Moffatt New Testament Commentary, New York Harper And Brothers, 1943.

16. The Book of Acts, Stanley M. Horton, Gospel Publishing House, 1981.

17. What Meaneth This? Carl Brumback, Gospel Publishing House, 1947.

18. Cruciality of the Cross, P.T. Forsyth M.A., D.D. Hodder and Stoughton, 1909

19. The Work of Christ, P.T. Forsyth M.A., D.D. Hodder and Stoughton, 1910.

20. Person and Work, B.B. Warfield, P & R Publishing, January 1950.

21. The Cross of Christ, John R. W. Stott, InterVarsity Press, 1986.

22. Spiritual Gifts, Melvin L. Hodges, Gospel Publishing House, 1964.

23. Hot Potatoes Christians are Afraid to Touch, by Tony Campolo, Thomas Nelson, January 1993.

24. William Smith Bible Dictionary, Hendrickson Publishers; Rev Sub edition, July 1, 1990.

25. The Twofold Life, A.J. Gordon, D. D. Hodder & Stoughton, 1910.

26. Science and Christian Tradition. Essays by T. H. Huxley, London: Macmillan & Co., 1894.

27. Modern Doubt on the Christian Faith, Theodor Christlieb, Bonn (2nd edition), 1870.

28. Panton, D. M Schoettle Pub. Co., 1988.

29. Wesley's Explanatory Notes on the Whole Bible, Baker Publishing Group (MI), December 1983.

30. 1st and 2nd Corinthians: An Ironside Expository Commentary, Kregel Academic & Professional; 1 edition, February 1, 2006.

31. The Man Who Presumed; a Biography of Henry M. Stanley, Farwell, Byron, (1957).

32. The New SchaffHerzog Encyclopedia of Religious Knowledge (13 Volumes), by Philip Schaff, J. J.Herzog, Albert Hauck, and Samuel Macauley Jackson, 1950.

33. Miraculous Healing, Henry W. Frost, D.D., Home Director Emeritus for North America, China Inland Mission, March 3, 1934, issue of the Sunday School Times.

34. Smith Wigglesworth: Apostle of Faith. Springfield, MO: Gospel Publishing House, Frodsham, Stanley Howard, 1948.

35. Agape Road: Journey to Intimacy with the Father, Bob Mumford, Life Changers Library, Destiny Image Publishers, March I, 2006.

36. The Elijah Task, John and Paula Sandford, Logos international, 1977.

There are many others that have been named within the pages of this work that at this time I would like to thank for their excellent contributions that help set the foundation of the wisdom needed to write this text. And also, to everyone that has taken the time to read the material contained within its pages I would also like to send my deepest heart felt thank you. May the Lord make His face shine upon thee, and be gracious unto thee: The Lord lift up his countenance upon thee, and give thee peace! Amen!

NOTES

Are The Gifts Of The Spirit For Today?

1. Henry W. Frost, D.D., Miraculous Healing, *The Sunday School Times*, March 3, 1934.
2. Johann Albrecht Bengel, *Harmony of the Four Gospels*, (published by Philip David Burk 1763).
3. Theodor Christlieb, *Modern doubt on the Christian faith*, (Bonn, and edition 1870).
4. D. M. Panton, The Panton Papers Current events and prophecy, a selection of editorial articles, (Schoettle Pub. Co 1988).
5. John Wesley, *Wesley's Explanatory Notes on the Whole Bible*, (Baker Publishing Group, MI, December 1983).
6. Dr. Harry A. Ironside, *I and 2 Corinthians: An Ironside Expository Commentary*, (Kregel Academic & Professional; 1 edition February 1, 2006).

Tongues In Regards To The Baptism Of The Holy Spirit

7. Dr. R. A. Torrey, *What the Bible Teaches*, (Hendrickson Publishers; New Ed edition November 1, 1998.)
8. Harold Horton, *The Gifts of the Spirit*, (Radiant Books 1934).

9. Doremus Almy Hayes, *The Synoptic Gospels and the Book of Acts*, (The Methodist Book Concern New York, 1919).
10. Philip Schaff, J. J. Herzog, Albert Hauck, and Samuel Macauley Jackson, *The New SchaffHerzog Encyclopedia of Religious Knowledge* (13 Volumes) (Baker Book House, 1951)
11. Matthew Henry, **Matthew Henry's Commentary**, (MacDonald Publishing 1706).

The Classification And Motivation Of Spiritual Gifts

12. Harold Horton, *The Gifts of the Spirit*, (Radiant Books 1934).

The Gifts Of Power

13. Stanley Howard Frodsham, Smith Wigglesworth: Apostle of Faith, (Gospel Publishing House 1948).
14. Kenneth Hagan, **The Holy Spirit and His Gifts**, (Rhema Bible Church, 1991).
15. T. H. Huxley, **Science and Christian Tradition, Essays by T H. Huxley**, (London: Macmillan 8z., Co., 1894).
16. Daniel Webster, **The New Lexicon Webster's. Dictionary of the English Language**, (Lexicon Publications, Inc. revised, 1989).
17. Herbert Lockyer, **All the Miracles of the Bible**, (Zondervan Books, 1961).
18. Harold Horton, **The Gifts of the Spirit**, (Radiant Books, 1934).
19. Frederic Louis Godet, **Commentary of I Corinthians**, (Kregel Publications', 1977).
20. Smith Wigglesworth, **Ever Increasing Faith,** (Gospel Publishing House, Revised edition, June 1971).
21. Smith Wigglesworth, **Ever Increasing Faith,** (Gospel Publishing House, Revised edition, June 1971).

22. James Strong, LL.D., S.T.D, *The New Strong's Exhaustive Concordance of the Bible*, (Thomas Nelson Publications, 1984).

23. Merrill F. Unger, *Unger's Bible Dictionary*, (Moody Press, 1987).

24. Don Basham, **Tongues, Interpretation, & Prophecy**, (Whitaker House, 1971).

25. William Smith, **William Smith's Bible Dictionary**, (Hendrickson Publishers; Rev Sub edition, July 1, 1990).

Apostles

26. A. J. Gordon, *The twofold life*, (DD Hodder & Stoughton, I884)

Prophets

27. Bob Mumford, **Agape Road. Journey to Intimacy with the Father**, (Life Changers Library, Destiny Image Publishers)

28. Rick Joyner, **Morning Star Journal**, Vol.5, No. 2, (Morning Star Publications, 1995).

29. Rick Joyner, **Morning Star Journal**, Vol.5, No. 2, (Morning Star Publications, 1995).

Evangelists

30. Karl Mark & Frederick Engles, *The Communist Manifesto, **Marx/Engels Selected Works, Volume One***, (Progress Publishers, Moscow, USSR, 1969).

31. Dr. D. James Kennedy, **Evangelism Explosion**, (Tyndale House Publishers Wheaton III. 1970).

32. Tony Campolo, *Hot Potatoes Christians are afraid to Touch*, (Thomas Nelson, January 1993).

33. Henry Morton Stanley, *How I Found Livingstone, Travels, Adventures and Discoveries in Central Africa*, (Scribner, Armstrong & Co., 1872).

34. Byron Farwell, *The Man Who Presumed; a Biography of Henry M. Stanley*, (Longmans, Green, 1958).

Helps And Administrations

35. Fenton John Anthony Hort, *The New Testament in the Original Greek*, (Brooke Foss Westcott, 1907).

36. Merrill F. Unger, *Unger's Bible Dictionary*, (Moody Press, 1987).

37. James Strong, LL.D., S.T.D, *The New Strong's Exhaustive Concordance of the Bible*, (Thomas Nelson Publications, 1984).

38. Frederic Louis Godet, *Commentary of I Corinthians*, (Kregel Publications', 1977).

39. Jamison, Fausset, & Brown, *A Commentary, Critical, Experimental, and Practical*, (Wm. B. Eerdmans Publishing Co., 1973).

40. Matthew Henry, Matthew Henry's Commentary, (MacDonald Publishing, 1706).

Love: Part One

41. P.T. Forsyth, *Cruciality of the Cross*, (Wipf & Stock Publishers, January 1, 1997).

42. P.T. Forsyth, *The Work of Christ*, (Wipf & Stock Publishers, July 1, 1996).

43. B.B. Warfield, *The Person and Work of Christ*, (Presbyterian Reformed Pub. Co., 1950).

44. John R.W. Stott, *The Cross of Christ*, (Intervarsity Press, 1986).